John Tucker

111 Places
in Richmond
That You
Must Not Miss

Photographs by Ashley Tucker

T0243748

emons:

To our moms and dads, for encouraging us to go exploring.

Bibliographical information of the Deutsche Nationalbibliothek
The Deutsche Nationalbibliothek lists this publication in
the Deutsche Nationalbibliografie; detailed bibliographical data
are available on the internet at http://dnb.d-nb.de.

© Emons Verlag GmbH
All rights reserved
© Photographs by Ashley Tucker, except see page 238
© Cover icon: shutterstock/Griffin Gillespie
Layout: Anja Sauerland, based on a design
by Lübbeke | Naumann | Thoben
Maps: altancicek.design, www.altancicek.de
Basic cartographical information from Openstreetmap,
© OpenStreetMap-Mitwirkende, OdbL
Edited by: Karen E. Seiger
Printing and binding: Grafisches Centrum Cuno, Calbe
Printed in Germany 2024
ISBN 978-3-7408-2002-2
First edition

Guidebooks for Locals & Experienced Travelers
Join us in uncovering new places around the world at
www.111places.com

Foreword

It hasn't always been cool for Richmonders to love their city. For much of my life, despite its captivating history and immediate access to the natural world, Richmond was treated with equal parts affection and disparagement by its residents. To be fair, the self-loathing came easily: the river was polluted, crime was high, minor league teams were repeatedly replaced with teams of yet lower stature, and that cringeworthy "Capital of the Confederacy" moniker we earned in 1861 remained all too celebrated. We secretly loved the city nonetheless; to use an old saying, Richmond might have been a bad dog, but it was *our* bad dog.

Then, through the tireless efforts of our citizens, good things began to happen here. The river got cleaned up. Crime went down. The museums underwent renovations. Commerce began to flourish. We learned how to acknowledge our transgressions without glorifying them. VCU went to the Final Four. Between the cracks of our reputation as a conservative, old-money, Southern town grew eccentric and subversive gems scattered throughout our neighborhoods. These little spots nurtured a fierce counterculture featuring famous death metal bands, world-renowned murals, quirky vintage shops, and an edgy culinary and craft beer scene. The history and nature that always elevated the city are still here, now with a dynamic and diverse culture to complement them. The 111 places described within these pages represent the tapestry of everything, old and new, that makes Richmond special.

Just as it was rebuilt after Benedict Arnold burned it down, and again when the Confederates did the same, Richmond is experiencing a period of rebirth. Our hidden gem has begun to shine a little brighter, and outsiders are seeing what we've known all along but have hesitated to admit: our city is amazing. It may never be cool to say, but I'm going to do it anyway – Richmond, I love you.

111 Places

1 Abuelita's

This is your grandmother's Mexican

"Food is *so* important to my family," says Karina Benavides, owner of Abuelita's, and she attributes this fact largely to the women featured in the weathered photographs on the walls of her restaurant. These are her *abuelitas*, the Mexican grannies who passed the tradition of culinary excellence onto her. In the small town in Jalisco where Benavides and her husband grew up, there weren't really restaurants. Food was lovingly served to the community in its living rooms. The decor of this restaurant, with doilies and terracotta *cazuelas*, or cooking pots, artfully arranged on the walls, is meant to conjure that feeling of familial informality, setting the scene of a home-cooked meal.

Abuelita's was born in 2017 from its founders' drive to cook the food they want to eat, which means the signature dishes of Western Mexico: *birria* (slow cooked beef), cactus salad, *pozole* (pork bone and hominy soup), and, in particular, the rotation of stews called *guisos,* served with rice, beans, and homemade corn tortillas. Every day, Abuelita's offers eight *guisos*, brightly colored and steaming, selected from over 20 recipes in the rotation.

Benavides points out that traditional cuisine remains so important to today's Mexican culture that it is one of two countries, along with France, whose food is recognized by UNESCO's Intangible Cultural Heritage program. Tracing its ancestry to ancient agricultural and cooking skills, traditional Mexican cuisine uses a diverse array of native ingredients missing from most American Mexican menus catering to tastes that evolved outside of Mexico. Abuelita's is a rare exception.

"We made a decision not to put the word 'Mexican' on the sign because we didn't want people to be disappointed when they see something different than what they're used to," said Benavides. So if you're looking for new and different types of *delicias* to enjoy, Abuelita's welcomes you home.

Address 6400 Midlothian Turnpike, Richmond, VA 23225, +1 (804) 997-2602, www.abuelitasrva.com | Getting there Bus 1A to Midlothian Pike & Warwick Road | Hours Tue–Sat 11am–8:30pm, Sun 11am–8pm | Tip The Perkinson Center for the Arts and Education hosts, among many other programs, the Latin Ballet of Virginia, the state's premier Pan-Latin dance company and school (11810 Centre Street, Chester, www.perkinsoncenter.org).

2 All Faiths Chapel

It's not the size of your chapel…

There's a truckload of lore surrounding the Doswell Truck Stop. Once billed as the "World's Busiest Truck Stop," the complex hosted the trucking industry's most popular radio DJ, "Big John" Trimble for two decades. In the early 1970s, a horse trainer from neighboring Meadowbrook Farms solicited a group of media executives having lunch at the diner here to invest in a promising young thoroughbred. They politely declined. That horse was named Secretariat.

Around 1990, a young country singer by the name of Alan Jackson was hanging out between sets at the truck stop lounge called Geraldine's, when he leaned too hard against a jukebox with a missing leg. "Don't rock the jukebox," his bassist admonished him, and a No. 1 hit was born.

For every legend passed down, though, there are several that fade with the passage of time, and so it is with the pint-sized tabernacle called the All Faiths Chapel tucked into the corner of the motel parking lot. The chapel was likely built by the original owner, Oran V. Jarrell, aka "God's Truckstop Man," although the date remains a mystery. A *Washington Post* article from 1978 references the chapel, noting that it showed "videotapes of six-minute sermons for Protestants, Catholics, Jews and the deaf."

The little chapel is approximately 20 by 12 feet and consists of a nave containing four pews leading to a small sanctuary. The space is cozy and peaceful, dim but for the light through eight stained glass windows, quiet but for the dulcet hum of traffic on Interstate-95. These days, Clint Bivins, former trucker and Army chaplain turned minister to the trucking community, leads the congregation at All Faiths. Mr. Bivins manages the facility, keeping it open throughout the week to welcome any truckers passing through to step in for some spiritual respite between long hauls. He also leads Bible study here on Thursday evenings.

Address 10222 Kings Dominion Boulevard, Doswell, VA 23047, www.allfaithschapel. squarespace.com, truckers.pray@gmail.com | **Getting there** By car, take I-95 North and take exit 98 for Kings Dominion | **Hours** Daily 8am–6pm | **Tip** From the tiny chapel, you can spot the tallest structure in Doswell, the one-third replica of the Eiffel Tower at neighboring Kings Dominion amusement park. At 315 feet tall, the tower provides an unparalleled view of the countryside north of Richmond (16000 Theme Park Way, Doswell, www.kingsdominion.com).

3 Aluminaut

Unlikely hero of the deep seas

The Reynolds Metal Company, a pioneer of aluminum foil, was one of Richmond's flagship manufacturing firms for the better part of the 20th century. In 1964, to show off the versatility and durability of aluminum, the company commissioned the world's first aluminum submarine, an 80-ton, five-foot-long cylinder called the *Aluminaut*.

The little, blue-and-yellow seacraft, with its bulbous nose and viewports that look like googly eyes, appears more like a toddler's bath toy than the serious, gun-metal gray subs from *Das Boot* or *The Hunt for Red October*. A 1964 *Time Magazine* article described it as "looking for all the world like a fat headed sperm whale." Despite its silly appearance and origins from a clever marketing campaign, the sub went on to have an impressive career in deep sea recovery and exploration.

In 1966, the *Aluminaut* helped recover a hydrogen bomb that had fallen to the bottom of the Mediterranean after a B-52 bomber crashed off the coast of Spain. Two years later, the submarine recovered a 2,100-pound torpedo that sank near the Bahamas. In 1969, the *Aluminaut* accomplished what was the deepest recovery dive in history when it salvaged a fellow submersible, the US Navy's DSV *Alvin*, from 6,000 feet beneath the Atlantic Ocean south of Nantucket. Apart from its heroics rescuing bombs and boats from the ocean floor, the *Aluminaut* also enjoyed a bit of fame from appearing in the films of oceanographer Jacques Cousteau (1910–1997).

In 1970, the submarine was retired and donated to the Science Museum of Virginia, where it remains on permanent, though not quite prominent, display. Unlike the sexier SR-71 Blackbird supersonic jet suspended from the museum's first-floor ceiling, the *Aluminaut* sits in the museum's backyard, beyond the old train sheds, where visitors could easily miss it. If you find it, give the little badass bomb-hunter a well-deserved salute.

Address 2500 W Broad Street, Richmond, VA 23220, +1 (804) 864-1400, www.smv.org |
Getting there Bus 20, 50, 76 to Robinson & Broad Streets, Pulse to Science Museum |
Hours Daily 9:30am–5pm | Tip Next door to the Science Museum is the Children's
Museum of Richmond, which offers a number of hands-on interactive exhibits and a
magnificent carousel (2626 W Broad Street, www.childrensmuseumofrichmond.org).

4 The Aquarian

Let's get metaphysical

Over its 41 years, the Aquarian has evolved from a small bookstore into Richmond's premier clearinghouse for items and services metaphysical. The shop recently expanded into two storefronts, one in the Fan and one in Carytown, paired like yin and yang right in the heart of Richmond.

The Carytown location is open, bright, and sparkly, literally, with its selection of giant, glistening geodes. It is also here where a fleet of psychics, clairvoyants, palm readers, tarot readers, empaths, astrologers, and numerologists meets with clients to foresee the future or connect with a hidden past.

The Main Street location has a slightly darker vibe and is most notable for its large apothecary. Between the counter and wooden shelves holding innumerable jars of herbs and essential oils, a pair of alchemists are hard at work, one helping a customer identify the perfect remedy, another using dropper bottles to prepare a tincture. A catalog on the counter lists hundreds of offerings delineated into categories, like cleansing waters, spiritual bath salts, mojo bags, honey pots, and house-blended conditioning powders for different purposes, including fertility, money drawing, love uncrossing, evil be gone, and jinx removal, among many others.

The Aquarian provides a sanctuary for Richmonders with belief systems outside the mainstream and for those who are curious about alternative viewpoints. Until the pandemic, the store hosted the Virginia Festival of Psychics, the largest gathering of soothsayers on the East Coast. They recently revived the annual Running of the Cones, a footrace of individuals wearing cone-shaped costumes in a shout-out to sacred geometry. Per the store's manager Nick Lasky, the Aquarian embraces Gnosticism, the idea that the metaphysical is directly accessible to everyone, and seeks to facilitate that access for those with an open mind.

Address 12 S Thompson Street, Richmond, VA 23221, +1 (804) 354-5501, www.aquarianbookshop.com, shop@aquarianbookshop.com | Getting there Bus 5, 78 to Ellwood Avenue & Nansemond Street | Hours Daily 11am–7pm | Tip Ellwood Thompson's, just across the parking lot from the Aquarian in Carytown, has been spearheading Richmond's organic and local foods movement since 1989. Like Aquarian, the store has evolved over the years from a simple market into an experience, all while maintaining its core values (4 N Thompson Street, www.ellwoodthompsons.com).

5 Arthur Ashe Tunnel

A colorful tribute to Richmond's favorite son

Let's go ahead and get it out there. Contrary to its own website, Battery Park is not where Arthur Ashe (1943–1993) learned to play tennis. The park did exist in Ashe's heyday, and it did have tennis courts, but Moe Thacker, his teammate at Maggie Walker High School, lived adjacent to the park and recalled in a 2018 interview with *Richmond Magazine* that there were not even nets on the courts between 1948 and 1960.

Tragically, the courts where Ashe actually did learn to play no longer exist. Nearby Brook Field Park was one of the few recreational sites for Richmond's Black citizens in the 1950s. Like many Black landmarks in the city, Brook Field Park was shut down in the 1960s to make way for another municipal project. "Looking back at my childhood, I see my world defined as a series of concentric circles," Ashe wrote in the *Washington Post* in 1981. "At the center was our house at 1610 Sledd Street. The next circle was Brook Field, which played an important role in defining my future."

Battery Park, however, is remarkable in its own right. Sitting in the predominantly Black neighborhood of Barton Heights, not far from Ashe's stomping grounds, the park now contains ten very well maintained tennis courts, nets and all, in addition to basketball courts, horseshoe pits, a swimming pool, and two playgrounds.

Most notably, the park features a memorial to Arthur Ashe in the form of brightly colored murals adorning the interior of a tunnel and both of its openings. One opening features a portrait of the young champion hoisting his Wimbledon trophy. Inside the tunnel, the major events of his life are listed in chronological order. The tunnel empties to another mural portraying an older, more solemn, bespectacled Ashe opposite the words he spoke and lived by, "From what we get, we can make a living; what we give, however, makes a life."

Address 2803 Dupont Circle, Richmond, VA 23222, +1 (804) 646-0944, www.rva.gov/parks-recreation/battery-park | Getting there Bus 1 to Chamberlaynes & Hammond Avenues | Hours Daily dawn–dusk | Tip Jackson Ward is home to a memorial for another of Richmond's favorite sons, vaudeville performer Bill "Bojangles" Robinson (1878–1949). His birthday, May 25th, is celebrated as National Tap Dance Day (601 Price Street, www.nps.gov/places/bill-bojangles-robinson-statue.htm).

6   B.A. Sunderlin Bellfoundry
Where the ringing all begins

To most people, the chime of a bell is the definition of background noise, a bit of faint, ubiquitous, clangor striking the subconscious with no particular significance. When you have watched a bell pouring, however, the process by which molten bronze and tin are carefully poured into a mold to become a bell, your appreciation for that sound is elevated. Due to the dwindling number of bell foundries worldwide, this experience is only available in the US in St. Louis, Cincinnati, and the small town of Ruther Glen, Virginia, where you will find the site of B.A. Sunderlin Bellfoundry, about 30 minutes north of Richmond.

When Ben Sunderlin first took an interest in bell-making as an undergraduate student in Indiana, he encountered a problem. In the US, there was no formal instruction in the craft and few opportunities for mentorship. He traveled abroad, first to England and then to France, where he learned the traditional methods of loam-molding used in Europe for hundreds of years. Sunderlin is now the only American bellfounder employing these traditional methods, utilizing a concoction of clay, sand, horse manure, and human hair to craft the mold into which the alloy is poured.

Kate Sunderlin, Ben's wife, is an art historian and manages the front-of-house activities at the foundry, including weekly tours on Thursdays. The tours begin in a small museum at the front of the facility dedicated to the history and science of campanology, the study of bells. Visitors then walk through the foundry itself and learn about the labor-intensive process of bellfounding, from design to molding to pouring to tuning, all of which happens in that one giant room.

Finally, guests gather for the big event. Through supplied sunglasses, you'll watch the soothing, incandescent, orange glow of molten metal flow into a mold like lava down the side of a volcano, as a brand new, baby bell is born.

Address 22537 Coleman's Mill Road, Ruther Glen, VA 22546, +1 (804) 448-0565, http://www.sunderlinfoundry.com | Getting there By car, take I-95 North to exit 104 onto SR-207 East, turn right onto Dry Bridge Road, and left onto Coleman's Mill Road. | Hours Mon–Fri 9am–5pm, weekends by appointment only | Tip If you love the sound of bells ringing, visit the Carillon at Dogwood Dell, a 240-foot tower housing 53 bronze bells played by a *carillonneur*. The tower is a memorial to the 3,700 Virginians who lost their lives in World War I (1300 Blanton Avenue, www.carilloncivic.org/index.php).

7 Babe's Volleyball Court

Hidden oasis at the country's oldest lesbian bar

In March 1984, at the height of an era known for municipal crackdowns on establishments hospitable to gay patrons and staff, Rosa Denby took over the space at 3166 West Cary and transformed what had been Babe's Steakhouse into Babe's of Carytown. The bar was and remains open to all walks of life but caters primarily to a gay, female clientele. At the time, there were approximately 200 other lesbian bars in the United States. According to the "Lesbian Bar Project," that number has dwindled to the low thirties, and Babe's is the oldest among those in existence.

Babe's is a cavernous, multifaceted space, with a U-shaped bar separating wooden, diner-style booths from the smoke and lasers of the large dance space, formerly a T-shirt shop. Through a narrow hallway and up a set of stairs, you emerge into the open-air cabana out back. There, in perhaps the greatest moment for LGBTQIA+ beach volleyball since copiously oiled Maverick and Goose squared off against Iceman and Slider to Kenny Loggins' "Playing with the Boys" in *Top Gun* (1986), a regulation-sized beach volleyball court added sometime in the early '90s. Concealed by an eight-foot privacy fence, the court is completely hidden to passersby ambling along Auburn Avenue, none-the-wiser until a killshot gone awry makes its way over the fence.

According to owner Vicky Hester, who has worked here since the mid-80s and bought the bar in 1999, the volleyball court was born out of necessity. She says that her clientele have always been intertwined with the Richmond sports leagues, but for years, the volleyball folks had nowhere to play. "Humphrey Calder and Byrd Park hosted just about everything else you can name, but there was no volleyball net, so we built the court." Over 30 years later, it remains a fixture for rec leagues around the city and those seeking a pickup match, particularly employees from neighboring Carytown bars.

Address 3166 W Cary Street, Richmond, VA 23221, +1 (804) 355-9330,
www.facebook.com/babesofcarytown | Getting there Bus 5, 78 to Cary & McCloy Streets |
Hours Wed & Thu 4pm–1am, Fri noon–2am, Sat 4pm–2am, Sun noon–9pm | Tip
Offering up legs and eggs on Saturdays and Sundays since 1997, Godfrey's nightclub and
restaurant hosts one of the country's oldest drag brunches. Like Babe's, Godfrey's has been
a beacon of inclusivity for Richmond's LGBTQIA+ community for decades (308 E Grace
Street, www.godfreysva.com).

8_ Belgian Building
An architectural relic hiding in plain sight

The charming miniature castles at Virginia Union University, members of the "nine noble buildings" erected in 1899 when the campus moved to its current Northside location, are among the prettiest buildings in Richmond. Constructed of slate, Virginia granite, and Georgia pine, these little fortresses feature flourishes like turrets and Romanesque arches that give the campus the cohesive and enduring character befitting the school's prominence and long history.

Richmonders are likely more familiar with the austere, gray tower rising 150 feet above the campus, though, given its visibility from the I-95/I-64 corridor. The structure supports a slatted cube so nondescript that to the unassuming eye, it could be mistaken as the housing for an air conditioning unit. In typical Richmond fashion, there is a hidden history to this building.

The tower was the centerpiece of the Belgian exhibit at the 1939 World's Fair in New York. The Belgians had intended to ship the installation back home at the event's closing, but by that time, the Nazis had occupied the region. Belgium instead put the installation up for sale and selected VUU from the 27 universities that bid for it. In addition to the tower and the cube, the installation included a ceramic bas-relief frieze at the bottom called *Belgians at Work*, featuring scenes of indigenous African people toiling in the Congo, which remained under Belgian colonization at the time that the building was donated.

VUU is a Historically Black College and one with a particularly captivating origin. Founded at the close of the Civil War inside the former jail building for enslaved people on the "Devil's Half-Acre" in downtown Richmond, the school may have been chosen by the Belgians as a gesture of reconciliation for its own brutal treatment of African people. The structure is fittingly known as the Belgian Friendship Building.

Address 1500 N Lombardy Street, Richmond, VA 23220, +1 (804) 257-5600, www.vuu.edu | Getting there Bus 14 to Lombardy & Admiral Streets | Hours Unrestricted | Tip The primary library at VUU was once housed in the Belgian Building but has moved to the L. Douglas Wilder Library, which displays a wide array of African and African American Folk Art (1500 N Lombardy Street, www.vuu.edu/library).

9 The Bent Spike

A dark curiosity at Old City Hall

Surrounding much of Old City Hall on downtown Broad Street stands a black, wrought-iron fence, similar to many others leftover from the Victorian Age in Richmond. But this particular fence has one small distinction. Near the northwest corner, the tine of one spire is bent backwards ever so slightly. It's the kind of mundane detail you would almost certainly not notice, unless you had heard the tragic tale that led to this minor imperfection.

Around 8:15am on August 23, 1894, an 11-year-old boy named Willie Dunford was standing at the corner of 9th & Broad when he noticed something odd. An elderly man was standing on the balcony of the clock tower of City Hall. One by one, according to the boy, the man threw the items in his possession - his cane, his hat, and his shoes - off the balcony. Then he stepped onto the balustrade and threw himself off.

Another eyewitness, Henry Brown, also reported seeing the man jump from the tower. A few others saw the lower part of the fall, and dozens more ran over to witness the aftermath, the remains of the man impaled on a single bent spike of the wrought iron fence below. From the documents found on his person, the unfortunate individual was identified as Colonel J.M. Winstead, a prominent banker from Greensboro, North Carolina.

Several newspapers covered the dreadful event in gruesome detail, but there are discrepancies among their reports, particularly with regard to the cause of the fall. The Virginia newspapers largely covered the fall as an obvious suicide, while the North Carolina papers indignantly rebutted this assertion with their own theory that Colonel Winstead's vertigo was to blame. Whatever evidence may have illuminated the circumstances of his death may not have withstood the sands of time, but 125 years later, the lone bent spike continues to serve as a grim reminder of the tragic incident.

Address 1001 E Broad Street, Richmond, VA 23219, +1 (804) 646-7000 | Getting there
Bus 1A, 1B, 1C, 7A, 7B, 56 to Broad & 12th Streets | Hours Unrestricted | Tip Perhaps
the best view of Old City Hall, and the rest of downtown Richmond, is from the 18th
floor observation deck of New City Hall across Broad Street (900 East Broad Street,
www.rva.gov).

10   Berkeley Plantation
Site of America's first Thanksgiving

A warning to any prideful New Englanders out there: The following sentence may upset you. The first English Thanksgiving in the US occurred at what is now called Berkeley Plantation, 21 miles southeast of Richmond, on December 4th, 1619, nearly two years before the Pilgrims feasted with the Wampanoag Indians at Plymouth. Lest there be any concern for ambiguity, read the declaration by John Woodlief, captain of the ship that moored there on that day following a treacherous, 80-day journey across the Atlantic: "wee ordaine that the day of our ships arrivall at the place assigned for plantacon in the land of Virginia shall be yearly and perpetualy keept holy as a day of thanksgiving to Almighty god."

That said, the events of that day bear little resemblance to the Thanksgiving that modern, gravy-guzzling Americans know and love. There was no feast and no involvement of the Native Americans at the Berkeley Thanksgiving. Much to the contrary, the tradition abruptly ended with the decimation of the settlement in the so-called Indian Massacre of 1622. Modern-day Berkeley inhabitants resurrected the annual celebration in 1958.

In addition to having hosted the first Thanksgiving, Berkeley celebrates a few other claims to fame. It's the site of the first distillation of bourbon in the United States. It's home to two American presidents and the site where "Taps" was first played. Visitors are welcome to tour the ancient grounds, which featured prominently in the arrival of the British to the New World, the Revolutionary War, and the Civil War. Harboring four centuries of this rich history is a verdant exterior with terraces sloping down to a small brick memorial honoring the 36 men who knelt and gave thanks in 1619. On a crisp, fall day, the setting is perfect for a picnic. The recommended fare would be turkey, stuffing, and a side of cranberry, of course.

Address 12602 Harrison Landing Road, Charles City, VA 23030, +1 (804) 829-6018, https://berkeleyplantation.com, info@berkeleyplantation.com | Getting there By car, take I-64 East to exit 200 onto I-295 South then take exit 22A onto SR-5 East, right onto Herring Creek Road, and left onto Harrison Landing Road | Hours Daily 9:30am – 4:30pm | Tip Head east on the Capital Trail, and you'll run into the Indian Fields Tavern and 5 Fields Brewing Company. Enjoy a beer and burger on the patio looking out over the centuries-old farms of Charles City (9220 John Tyler Memorial Highway, Charles City, www.indianfieldstavern.com).

11 Bertha's Country Lane

Bringin' the boondocks to the Fan

When long-time Fan resident and local legend Bertha Burke passed away in July 2022 at the age of 101, she left behind a legacy as wide as a country mile. Having grown up on a tobacco farm in Brunswick County, she called herself a country girl, accustomed to digging in the dirt. Despite her upbringing, as a young newlywed she found herself living in a rowhouse in the Fan, a densely populated grid somewhat lacking in space for planting. Undeterred by the constraints of city living, Burke got to work cultivating the biggest piece of property she could find there: the 100-foot alley adjacent to her house on North Belmont Avenue.

In 1954, Burke and her husband Milton placed some extra gravel they had left over from another project over the tire tracks in the alley behind their house and planted grass in between. She began growing a garden, first in her backyard and then in the alley, full of wisteria, roses, petunias, impatiens, camellias, and more. She transformed the alley into a verdant hideaway beloved to this day by neighbors in the Museum District.

On February 25th, 2013, the Richmond City Council unanimously passed City Ordinance 2013-31-28, formally recognizing Burke's efforts by naming the alley after her in recognition of her 70 years of dedication. What had been known informally for several decades was made official with a proper street sign, Fan emblem and all, reading "Bertha's Country Lane."

"The splendor of the alley grew into an urban garden masterpiece due to her kind attention and constant loving care," the ordinance read. "Mrs. Burke's outstanding dedication to creating and maintaining this community feature has created many admirers and the appreciation of her entire neighborhood." Since Burke's passing, community members have carried the mantle of maintaining her country lane, tending to the garden and the legacy of the woman who started it all.

Address 100 North Belmont Avenue, Richmond, VA 22301 | Getting there Bus 5, 78 to Belmont & Ellwood Avenues or bus 77 to Belmont & Groves Avenues | Hours Unrestricted | Tip Matching Bertha's Country Lane in its dimensions and quaintness, Belmont Food Shop just one block south offers excellent farm-to-table fare. The small space holds only five tables, creating an intimate, homey vibe (27 North Belmont Avenue, www.facebook.com/belmontfoodshop).

12 Birthplace of Secretariat
Big Red's old stomping grounds

In the wee hours of March 30, 1970, on a cold and rainy Virginia night, a very special horse was born. The setting was a small, blue and white shed on a Caroline County farm called the Meadows, about 25 miles north of Richmond. According to a sign beside the shed, when farm manager Howard Gentry delivered the foal's back legs, he reportedly exclaimed, "There's a whopper!" And hours later Dr. Olive Britt, the farm veterinarian, described the foal as "beautiful… as red as fire." Befittingly sired by Bold Ruler and delivered by Somethingroyal, the princely colt named Secretariat would go on to dominate the world of horseracing.

It was clear from the beginning that Secretariat was special. He was known to have a playful personality, and Gentry's nephew Robert described him as a "clown… always into some devilment." On the racetrack though, he didn't play around, winning 16 of his 21 races. He famously won the 1973 Triple Crown and set course records at all three tracks that still stand to this day. Also still standing are several of the landmarks at the Meadows that tell the story of Secretariat's early life, including the foaling shed where he was born, the meadow where he grazed as a foal, the yearling stables where he lived as a one-year-old, and the stables where he trained in the year prior to his Triple Crown victory.

The Meadows belonged to the Chenery family, who bred horses there from 1936-1979. Prior to Secretariat, the farm produced several other champions, including Racing Hall of Fame inductees Hill Prince, Cicada, and Riva Ridge, who won the Kentucky Derby and Belmont Stakes in 1972. The farm has largely been converted into a sprawling event space hosting the Virginia State Fair and other conventions but still maintains the original digs of its most famous former resident. You are welcome to take a self-guided tour available free of charge during weekdays.

Address 13191 Dawn Boulevard, Doswell, VA 23047, +1 (804) 994-2800, www.meadoweventpark.com | Getting there By car, take I-95 North to VA-30 and drive east to the destination | Hours Mon – Fri 9am – 5pm | Tip Another famous horse is buried east of Richmond at Sherwood Forest, the home of President John Tyler. Next to the grave is an epitaph written by Tyler that reads, "Here lies the body of my good horse, 'The General'. For 20 years he bore me around the circuit of my practice, and in all that time he never made a blunder. Would that his master could say the same!" (14501 John Tyler Memorial Highway, Charles City, www.sherwoodforest.org).

13 __ Black Rabbit Tattoo
Beacon in a sea of ink

According to a study conducted by totalbeauty.com in 2013, Richmond had the third largest number of tattoo shops per capita in the United States. Two years later, Kim Graziano opened Black Rabbit Tattoo, and the shop immediately stood apart for its bright atmosphere and unique values. In an era when the industry wasn't known for its hospitality to girly girls and anime aficionados, Black Rabbit opened its doors to these groups, carving out a colorful and vibrant niche amid a crowded landscape.

Early on, Black Rabbit attracted an all-female roster of tattoo artists seeking sanctuary from a toxic industry with a culture of hazing apprentices. The shop has since moved on from its explicit "all-girl" identity, but remnants of the vibe remain. These include the neon "GIRLS! GIRLS! GIRLS!" sign in the window and depictions of powerful female figures like buxom, blade-wielding manga warriors and cartoonish, callipygian bunnies saturating the painted-pink walls.

The shop also distinguished itself with a focus on fandom-centric art, welcoming an enormous subculture devoted to certain realms of pop culture, particularly Japanese-style animation, that other shops tended to ignore. As it turns out, nerds like tattoos too, and there are a lot of them. The melding of anime and tattoos may have grown without the influence of Black Rabbit, but Graziano certainly drove it forward by hosting the massive annual Anime Ink Con in downtown Richmond each October.

Black Rabbit has largely shed its "girl tattoo shop" and "anime tattoo shop" labels but continues to promote inclusivity and diversity in the world of body art. With a door open to walk-ins most days, depending on artist availability, the shop welcomes anyone to drop in, take a peek at the cheerful, colorful space, and maybe get some ink. As the sign above the register says, "If you don't belong… then you belong here."

@bunnymachine

Address 17 N Belmont Avenue, Richmond, VA 23221, +1 (804) 353-1002, www.instagram.com/black_rabbit_tattoo, blackrabbitrva@gmail.com | Getting there Bus 5, 78 to Ellwood & Belmont Avenues | Hours Daily 11am–7pm | Tip Visit another bright, fun space around the corner at Carytown's World of Mirth, the best toy store in Richmond (3005 W Cary Street, www.worldofmirth.com).

14 Blackbyrd Goods
Makers of Richmond's most stylish accessories

A culture of creativity in Richmond nurtures its entrepreneurs, the innovative souls who find a niche and pour themselves into their craft. Included among them is Patrick Pearson, founder of Blackbyrd Goods, a boutique in Carytown selling apparel and accessories designed and made on site. The store sells t-shirts, jeans, and hats, both its own creations and a curated collection of small, international brands, particularly from Iceland. However, the hallmark of the store is its unique, screen-printed, leather goods.

In the middle of the store is a comfortable, oaky lounge, imbued with the scent of leather and espresso. A mellow bassline vibrates through mid-century modern chairs, and richly varnished wooden furniture invites guests to sit and consider how the aesthetic here can complement their own lifestyle.

The warmth of the space is reflective of its owner. Pearson is a native Richmonder living by Byrd Park, from whence the store gets the clever tweak to its name. A one-time car salesman with all of the affability and none of the intrusiveness, Pearson began crafting wallets in his spare time and was pleased enough with the quality that he stopped hawking cars and decided instead to sell leather. He picked up the screen-printing part soon thereafter. "With the internet and an unlimited amount of coffee, you can teach yourself anything," he says.

Also included in the equation is enthusiasm for the lesson, and Pearson's passion for the process shines through at the store, so much so that customers are invited upstairs to see where the goods are made. "I've had people say, 'I love this belt, but I wish it were in red.' So I take them upstairs to the studio, and ten minutes later they've got the belt in red." In a small ecosystem of affordable, locally made goods, Blackbyrd is one of the rare specimens contributing to Richmond's unique commercial landscape.

Address 3439 W Cary Street, Richmond, VA 23221, +1 (804) 716-1789, www.blackbyrdgoods.com, patrick@blackbyrdgoods.com | Getting there Bus 5, 78 to Cary Street & Freeman Road | Hours Thu–Sat noon–6pm, Sun noon–4pm | Tip Just down the road from Blackbyrd is a trio of stores, Clementine, Clover, and Ashby, specializing respectively in upscale, second-hand, adult clothing, children's clothing, and home goods. They are key stops for shoppers strolling along Carytown's "Mile of Style" (3118 W Cary Street, www.shopclementinerva.com).

15   Blandford Church
Historic home to 15 Tiffany windows

Built in 1736, Blandford Church has witnessed some pivotal events in American history. During the Revolutionary War, Major General William Philips (c. 1731 – 1781) commanded the British troops that captured Petersburg but then died nearby of an unknown infection. Benedict Arnold (1741 – 1801), at this point, fighting for the British, ordered Philips's body buried at Blandford, where it remains in an unmarked grave.

During the Civil War, the building was used as a Confederate telegram office and military hospital amid the bloody siege of Petersburg. In the aftermath, the land adjacent was converted into a massive burial ground for around 30,000 Confederate soldiers, who died in nearby battles. A Decoration Day ceremony that occurred there in 1866 reportedly inspired the designation of Memorial Day as a federal holiday.

The site is best known these days for the 15 stained glass windows crafted by Louis Comfort Tiffany (1848 – 1933). In 1900, the Ladies Memorial Association, a group of women who fundraised for memorials to fallen Confederate soldiers, commissioned Tiffany to design the windows. To afford the $350 per window, the ladies assigned each one a Southern state to foot the bill. Kentucky declined the offer, but two border states, Maryland and Missouri, accepted.

Although the original motive behind the windows may have been to glorify the Southern cause in the Civil War and blend it with the righteousness of the saints depicted, their aesthetic appeal cannot be denied. The interior of the church is kept dark such that the sunlight accentuates the features of the windows, including details painted over the faces, hands, and feet of the saints and Tiffany's signature patterns in their garments. Blandford remains one of the finest showcases of the artist's talent. Set into a nearly 300-year-old building, the site is a remarkable convergence of art and history.

Address 111 Rochelle Lane, Petersburg, VA 23803, +1 (804) 948-4455, https:// visitpetersburgva.org/attractions/blandford-church-museum-cemetery | Getting there By car, take I-95 South to exit 51 onto I-85 South to exit 52, turn left onto Wythe Street, right onto S Crater Road, and left onto Rochelle Lane; bus PAT Freedom Express to Petersburg Transfer Station, then bus 460 to Little Church & Wythe Streets | Hours Thu–Sat 10am–4pm, Sun 1–4pm | Tip To see more Tiffany windows, visit St. Paul's Episcopal Church in Richmond. Look for pew No. 63, where Jefferson Davis sat when he learned that the Union army was on its way to capture Richmond (815 E Grace Street, www.stpaulsrva.org).

16   Blue Atlas
A new take on old school cuisine

How's this for a hot take: In a city known for its emerging culinary scene, Richmond's finest cuisine is made in an elementary school cafeteria, or, more precisely, the repurposed cafeteria of the former Robert Fulton Elementary School, which operated from 1916 to 1979. It is now home to the Blue Atlas Restaurant & Market.

In 1997, the schoolhouse was purchased and its 32 classrooms renovated into 50 artists' studios, rebranded collectively as Artisan Hill. In 2020, chef couple Rachel Best and Ben Watters took over two large former classrooms and converted one into an indoor restaurant and the other into an artisanal market. In between them, double doors lead to outdoor dining on a portico with the best sunset view in Richmond.

Best and Watters moved back to her hometown of Richmond from Boulder, Colorado, where she had specialized in vegetarian fare and he in French cuisine. Their landlord at the time just so happened to own the former schoolhouse in Richmond. "She joked that if we were ever thinking of moving back, she had the perfect space for us," said Watters. That "perfect space" had been converted into a splatter art studio and now resembled a giant Jackson Pollock canvas, but Best and Watters got to work cleaning it up. They opened in spring 2020, just in time for the global pandemic to bring the restaurant industry to its knees. "For us, it kind of worked out," Watters says. "Unlike other restaurants that had to pivot, we just got off the ground slow and steady."

Blue Atlas is named for a species of cedar tree native to the Mediterranean but also growing right here in the Fulton Hill schoolyard. The name also evokes the wide geographic range of the fare on the menu, which is separated into four categories: Americas, Middle East & Africa, Europe, and Asia. Next time you're hungry, go back to school for the city's most delicious geography lesson.

Address 1000 Carlisle Avenue, Suite 200, Richmond, VA 23231, +1 (804) 554-0258, www.blueatlasrva.com, info@blueatlasrva.com | **Getting there** Broad/Main/Rocketts to Rocketts Landing Station | **Hours** Wed–Sat 9am–9pm, Sun 9am–3pm & 5–8pm | **Tip** Head down Fulton Hill and across Williamsburg Road to enjoy some yard games and a Falcon Smash at Triple Crossing, one of Richmond's finest breweries (5203 Hatcher Street, www.triplecrossing.com/pages/fulton).

17 — Branch House Library

A reading nook circa the Gilded Age

On a cold, rainy day, the second-floor reading room at the Branch House is the coziest place to read a book. Running south to north, the vaulted ceiling stretches from oaken bookshelves flanking a big, sandstone fireplace, across pargeted, white, plaster ceilings supporting Hogwartian chandeliers, to leaded glass windows that look out onto cars splashing through puddles on Monument Avenue. As the library of the Museum of Architecture and Design, the bookshelves hold volumes dedicated to those topics, including studies of the works of John Russell Pope (1874–1937), architect of the Jefferson Memorial, the National Archives, National Gallery of Art, and, indeed, the Branch House itself.

The reading room is the subjective highlight of an objectively remarkable house. Built in an era when Anglophilia swept through Richmond, leaving in its wake Tudor and Jacobean mansions like Agecroft Hall and the Virginia House across town, the Branch House was commissioned by banker John Kerr Branch (1865-1930), baron of the Richmond banking industry. The 27,000-square-foot mansion, still the largest single-family home in Richmond, was built largely to house the Renaissance-era treasures that Branch and his family had amassed, paintings, suits of armor, tapestries and the like. The Branches themselves only spent the winter season at the house. They spent the rest of the year at estates in New York and Tuscany.

These days, the house is shared with the public. En route to the reading room, take a spin through the first-floor exhibit spaces, where ancient relics contrast with studies of contemporary design. A recent exhibit displayed posters depicting 21st-century Women's Rights campaigns from across the globe, contrasted with adjacent 15th-century, Italian chapel doors bearing handles in the shape of little, naked mermaids. You can join guided tours of the entire mansion.

Address 2501 Monument Avenue, Richmond, VA 23220, +1 (804) 655-6055,
www.branchmuseum.org, frontdesk@branchmuseum.org | Getting there Bus 20 to
Robinson & Broad Streets | Hours Tue–Sat 10am–5pm, Sun 1–5pm | Tip For a taste
of vintage Richmond cuisine, pick up a box lunch from Sally Bell's just around the corner
from the Branch House. Slinging their signature potato salad and cupcakes since the 1920s,
Sally Bell's was recognized as an American Classic by the James Beard Foundation in 2015
(2337 W Broad Street, www.sallybellskitchen.com).

18 Burlesque at Gallery5

Turn up the heat at Richmond's oldest firehouse

In 2005, Gallery5 moved into Jackson Ward's Steamer Company No. 5. Dating back to 1849, the building served as Richmond's first fire station, police station, and jail. The non-profit is dedicated to promoting freedom of expression and providing Richmond with a space to showcase unconventional, progressive, and cutting edge art. For years, one mainstay of Gallery5's mission has been a monthly burlesque show.

For an endeavor that celebrates the sultry, revels in the risqué, and basks in the bawdy, the event, entitled *AfroTease: The Cookout*, feels unexpectedly virtuous. One evening's emcee, Venessa Chevelle, warns the audience that, although they are expected to interact with the performers, the comfort and consent of all are integral parts of the show. The crowd is diverse, warm, welcoming, and inclusive. Body positivity is cooked into the whole experience by the performances of stars baring blemishes and plus-size beauty seemingly without any self-consciousness. Personal proclivities be damned – the result is 100% sexy.

Virtues aside, the positivity at the heart of the show is dressed down in a lacy gown of lust, libido, and licentious, lascivious lechery. "Who is a glutton?" the emcee inquires to a full-throated cheer. "Who likes an overabundance of sexual pleasures?" to yet louder applause. "Who is FERALLLLL?!?" The crowd loses their minds, and the emcee takes note, "You are giddy. You are fucking giddy." It's true; the giddy crowd hangs on her every word until appropriately warmed up for the next act.

It's hard to believe that the tiny, old firehouse can contain the energy of the 200 or so people packed into it, but it makes the performances that much more intimate. Once the evening is over, as everyone exits the gallery with big postcoital energy, another patron articulates the mood nicely, "Damn, I fell in love like 20 different times tonight."

Address 200 W Marshall Street, Richmond, VA 23220, www.gallery5arts.org, info@gallery5arts.org | Getting there Bus 3A, 3B, 3C, 14, 50, 78 to Broad & Adams Streets | Hours Fri & Sat 5–11pm | Tip Another renovated old firehouse, Station No. 10 on Broad Street, now belongs to the Firehouse Theater, one of the few companies performing original plays in Richmond (1609 W Broad Street, www.firehousetheatre.org).

19 Cannon at Drewry's Bluff

The gun that prolonged the Civil War

Atop a 90-foot cliff at Drewry's Bluff in Chester sits a giant cannon perched like a hawk with a single watchful eye over the river bend one mile to the East. The gun is an eight-inch Columbiad, a monster weighing in at 9,240 pounds and capable of firing a 65-pound shell a distance of two and a half miles. The cannon stood in that exact same location on May 15, 1862, the fateful day that an adversary rounded the river bend and laid anchor.

As part of the Peninsula Campaign of 1862, Union General George McClellan (1826 – 1885) sent five warships up the James River to test the naval approach to capturing Richmond. Recognizing the city's new vulnerability, Confederate strategists had scrambled together a rudimentary fortress atop Drewry's Bluff, which became the last line of defense against the two ironside warships, the USS *Galena* and USS *Monitor*, and three gunboats that sailed upriver that morning.

At 7:45am, the fleet sailed into Confederate view, and for almost four hours, they absorbed and delivered "the perfect tornado of shot and shell," according to the National Park Service website, including those fired by the three Columbiad cannons. Fourteen Union sailors and seven Confederate soldiers perished in the battle. Its munitions depleted, the *Galena* was rendered a "slaughterhouse," appearing as though it had survived "an attack of smallpox," per eyewitness accounts. The fleet retreated back downriver. The next time a Union ship passed under Drewry's Bluff would be April 4th, 1865, when the USS *Bat* carried President Abraham Lincoln (1809 – 1865) to Richmond to tour the recently captured city.

Aside from the cannon and its fortification, there's not much to suggest that Drewry's Bluff was ever more than a place to view the splendor of the James. Like other battlefields in the area, the setting these days is as rich an experience in Virginia's natural beauty as in its history.

Address 7600 Fort Darling Road, Richmond, VA 23237, +1 (804) 226-1981, https://www.nps.gov/rich/learn/historyculture/drewrys-bluff.htm | Getting there By car, take US-1 South, turn left onto Bellwood Road and left onto Fort Darling Road | Hours Daily 7am–6pm | Tip Downriver is City Point, the spot of land on which General Ulysses S. Grant spent the last year of the Civil War. President Lincoln spent two of the last three weeks of his life on the property, planning the end of the war. A small cabin used as Grant's headquarters still stands (1001 Pecan Avenue, Hopewell, www.nps.gov/pete/index.htm).

20 Church Hill Tunnel
Tragedy on the tracks

The C&O Railway tunnel, built in 1873, spans 10 city blocks underneath Church Hill. Practically from its inception, the tunnel was considered a safety hazard due mainly to the soft constitution of the material it cut through. It was shut down in 1901 because of these concerns, but in 1925 the company began renovating the tunnel to accommodate increased railroad traffic.

On October 2nd, 1925, tragedy struck downtown Richmond, when 150 feet of the tunnel collapsed, killing four men. In the days following the disaster, the tunnel was too precarious for rescue efforts, and two of the men remain entombed within it to this day, along with the Steam Locomotive No. 231.

Both ends of the tunnel were closed off but remain visible today. Sitting within a wooded ravine, the eastern end belongs in the opening chapter of a murder mystery, in which a seasoned detective passes under yellow tape to inspect a grisly crime scene. A stone wall within the tunnel seals off the site of the explosion, but the first 100 feet are closed off only by a flimsy chain link fence and flooded with murky brown water. Ironically, the far less creepy western end, which is neatly sealed off and visible from the street, provides the setting for Richmond's most haunting urban legend.

Based on the testimony of bystanders, shortly after the explosion of the steam engine that fateful day, a horrifying creature with beet-red eyes and skin peeling from its bones appeared at the western end of the tunnel. Like the mob that chased Frankenstein's monster, a group of curious Richmonders allegedly pursued the beast all the way from Church Hill to Hollywood Cemetery, where it crawled into the tomb of a Manchester man named W.W. Poole and never left. This mausoleum, according to legend, is the tomb of the Richmond Vampire, and curious souls visit the site regularly, hoping for a glimpse of the monster.

Address 401 N 18th Street, Richmond, VA 23223 | Getting there Bus 7A, 7B, 56 to Broad & 17th Streets or Broad & 18th Streets | Hours Unrestricted | Tip At the eastern end of Jefferson Park, under which the tunnel collapsed, sits a tiny shack called Alamo Barbecue, smoking some of the best barbecue Richmond has to offer (2202 Jefferson Avenue, www.alamobbq.com).

21 Cold Harbor & Gaines' Mill

The intersection of two Civil War campaigns

At the intersection of two country roads cutting through Hanover County, just 10 miles northeast of downtown Richmond, lies a historical marker with the following inscription:

> *Around this crossroads is bloody ground. To the right is the field of Gaines' Mill or First Cold Harbor, fought June 27, 1862, with 14, 800 casualties. To the left is Second Cold Harbor, near which 17,000 fell, May 30 - June 12, 1864.*

One hundred sixty years have passed since warfare twice brutalized this idyllic neighborhood, and it's so peaceful here these days that it requires effort to imagine the carnage that unfolded. Walking trails with historical placards wind by cannons and wooden, zigzag, battlefield fencing set up to provide some historical context. Silence has replaced gunfire, and green fields are empty of the 5,000 men who lay dead here in the aftermath of two of the war's bloodiest battles. Scars do remain though in the form of trenches dug deep into the earth by soldiers from both sides, serving as prompts to help visitors envision the harrowing descriptions of this place from the men that survived.

Both sides in the Civil War appreciated how absolutely vital Richmond was to the Southern cause. As the political capital of the Confederacy, the source of half of all Southern munitions, and the origin of five railway lines distributing those arms, the city was the linchpin of the Confederacy. Throughout the war, capturing Richmond was a primary objective of the Union, and defending it was paramount to Robert E. Lee (1807–1870) and his Confederate Army. These opposing interests culminated in two major Union campaigns to capture the city: the Peninsula Campaign of 1862 and the Overland Campaign of 1864. The two campaigns took different approaches to penetrating defenses around the city but intersected at this site, which is now protected as part of the Richmond Battlefields National Park.

Address 5515 Anderson-Wright Drive, Mechanicsville, VA 23111, +1 (804) 730-5025, www.nps.gov/rich/learn/historyculture/cold-harbor.htm | Getting there By car, take I-295 to Creighton Road north then turn right on Cold Harbor Road and left on Anderson-Wright Drive | Hours Wed–Sun 9am–4:30pm | Tip Many of the wounded men from both of these battles were transported to Church Hill and treated at Chimborazo Hospital, now the site of the Chimborazo Medical Museum (3215 E Broad Street, www.virginia.org/listing/chimborazo-medical-museum/6127).

22 The Crater

Petersburg's deepest wound

Physical reminders of the warfare that consumed the Richmond area during the Civil War remain abundant, but damage from the Battle of the Crater was so pronounced that the battle is literally named for the scars it left behind.

In June of 1864, Grant and the Union army arrived at Petersburg, where Lee and the Confederate army had established well-defended trenches that would be difficult to break. A Union coal mining engineer named Henry Pleasants proposed a clever plan to dig a mine from the Union trenches under the Confederate fortified position and set off an underground explosion, thereby creating an opening through enemy lines.

It took Union soldiers 24 days to dig a 586-foot-long mine, and another two weeks to prepare the explosives, all without detection by the enemy soldiers overhead. At 4:44am on July 30, 1864 the dynamite detonated, instantly killing 278 Confederate soldiers and blasting a crater into the earth measuring 170 feet long, 120 feet wide, and 30 feet deep. From there, things went horribly for the Union side. Faulty fuses, last minute personnel changes, and inept leadership (the two commanders overseeing the assault were observed getting drunk far away from the action) resulted in the slaughter of the Union soldiers, who rushed through the newly formed gap. Grant lost the opportunity to seize Petersburg and Richmond in August 1864 and spare both sides the nine more months of bloodshed that ultimately ensued.

In a letter he sent to Major General Henry Halleck, Grant later lamented the Battle of the Crater as "the saddest affair I have witnessed in this war."

When you visit the Petersburg National Battlefield, you can walk up to the entrance of the mine shaft, still outlined by the original granite stones set in place by the hands of Union soldiers, and follow the ruins of the mine depressed into the earth all the way to the Crater.

Address 1539 Hickory Hill Road, Petersburg, VA 23803, +1 (804) 732-3531, www.nps.gov/pete/learn/historyculture/battle-of-the-crater.htm | Getting there By car, take I-95 South to exit 50 on County Drive, then turn left onto Hickory Hill Road; bus PAT Freedom Express to Petersburg Transfer Station, then bus 460 to County Drive & Hickory Hill Road | Hours Daily 9am–8pm | Tip The Seven Days Battles of the Peninsula Campaign ended at Malvern Hill, a small knoll east of Richmond, where over 100,000 soldiers met in battle on July 1, 1862. The site is now part of the National Park Service, and the battlefields are considered the best preserved in Central Virginia (9175 Willis Church Road, www.nps.gov/rich/learn/historyculture/mhbull.htm).

23 _ Crossroads Art Center
A labyrinth of local culture

The greater Richmond area is home to approximately 50 institutions where art is displayed for purchase, a group ranging from polished galleries to accessible community exhibition spaces. Among these, Crossroads Art Center stands alone for its volume. Housed within a 25,000-square-foot building at Broad Street and Staples Mill Road, a block shared with its even larger neighbor, the behemoth West End Antiques Mall, Crossroads is a maze of captivating booths displaying the works of over 270 artists, almost all of them from Richmond or nearby.

"As far as I know, we're the largest for-profit gallery on the East Coast," says owner Jenni Kirby, a mosaic artist who opened the gallery in 2002. Kirby also has a business degree and identified a vacuum. A city known for its output of quality art did not have a proper marketplace to sell it locally. "A lot of high-end artists come out of VCU or teach there, but most of those people have gallery representation. There's a whole, huge next echelon of artists putting out fabulous art with nowhere else to sell it. We provide that middle market for consumers that want high-quality art but can't spend $20,000 or even $5,000 on a painting."

The layout is also accommodating to Richmond's youngest art connoisseurs. Realizing that there weren't many galleries displaying art for kids, Crossroads hosts several artists that cater to the walls of children's bedrooms. Many parents have noticed how the center's endless walls filled with art can keep an energetic child entertained. "People come through with strollers all the time, and we have a challenge for kids to find all the cows in the gallery." The sheer size of the space and the volume of works make for a unique art experience. You can spend hours losing yourself, literally and figuratively amidst the creativity. If you have time to kill and wall space to fill, Crossroads is the place to start.

Address 2016 Staples Mill Road, Richmond, VA 23230, +1 (804) 278-8950, www.crossroadsartcenter.com | **Getting there** Bus 18 to Staples Mill Road & W Marshall Street | **Hours** Tue–Sat 10am–5pm, Sun noon–4pm | **Tip** In case you haven't already gotten your steps in at Crossroads, head next door to browse for furnishings at the aforementioned neighboring West End Antiques Mall. At 53,000 square feet, the space dwarfs even Crossroads in volume (2004 Staples Mill Road, www.westendantiquemall.com).

24 The Cucumber Tree
The oldest living witness to Virginia history

Richmond is home to several very special trees. The Darlington Oak at Maymont is a national champion, meaning the largest of its species. Legend has it that Umpa the orange osage, who lives at Forest Hill Park, was planted from seeds sent eastward by Lewis & Clark to Thomas Jefferson. However, there is no Richmond-area tree more impressive than the *Magnolia acuminata* (cucumber tree) behind the Violet Bank House in Colonial Heights.

Under a 98-foot-wide canopy, a trunk 23 feet in circumference commands a shady sanctuary crisscrossed by low-hanging branches bending to the ground under their own weight like welcoming arms to visitors underneath. As the centerpiece of the community, this tree is a favorite spot for wedding photos and for pre-prom photos among high schoolers. Colonial Heights residents so revere the tree that its image comprises the emblem of the city's flag.

Believed to have been planted in 1718, the 300-year-old elder statesman has witnessed some of the most pivotal events in the nation's history. The original structure standing beside it, the Violet Bank House, served as the headquarters for the Marquis de Lafayette during the Revolutionary War. The tree also stood by while British and Colonial forces exchanged fire on this property during the Battle of Petersburg in 1781.

The house's foundation and two large chimneys survived a fire in 1810, and from these, the current structure was rebuilt from plans of Benjamin Latrobe (1764–1820), architect of the US Capitol building. During the Siege of Petersburg in 1864, the house was the headquarters of Robert E. Lee, who was known to hold church services under the tree. The blast that formed the Crater from the 1864 battle, two miles to the southeast, would have shaken the tree at its roots. If its branches could speak, the Cucumber Tree would be Professor Emeritus of American history.

Address 303 Virginia Avenue, Colonial Heights, VA 23834, +1 (804) 520-9395, www.colonialheightsva.gov/499/Violet-Bank | Getting there By car, take I-95 South to exit 54 to Temple Avenue, then turn right onto Conduit Road, right onto Ivey Avenue, left onto Cameron Avenue, and left onto Virginia Avenue; bus 95X to Petersburg Transfer Station and walk to destination | Hours Mon–Fri 10am–5pm, Sat 10am–4pm | Tip Another favorite local tree is Federal Park's Paper Mulberry, whose massive, knobby trunk held tributes to cyclist Robyn Hightman after their untimely death in 2020 (between Main Street, Floyd Avenue, Rowland Street, and Shields Avenue).

25 Dandelion Springs Apiary
See what the buzz is all about

Jody Conway is the owner and, if you will, queen bee of the Dandelion Springs Apiary, a honey farm just outside of Winterpock, VA, about 25 miles southwest of Richmond. The apiary now has 20 hives on 30 acres, but it traces its roots to Conway's more modest backyard operation in Carytown several years earlier.

The move certainly improved life for the bees. Bees need proper forage and the right habitat, ideally composed of native plants without chemicals, to make high quality honey, as Conway mentioned in the Saturday class, "Where do pollinators live?" Dandelion Springs is the perfect setting for the complex network of plants, insects, and animals, domesticated and wild, to make for happy bees.

The main reason for the move, though, was Conway's goal of hosting a teaching apiary, a space where the community could learn beekeeping and the sustainable farming practices necessary to do it well. On weekends, the farm hosts donation-based classes with a wide range of topics and intended audiences. One weekend, Conway hosted "Who's who on the farm," where kids met the resident horses, goats, sheep, chickens, ducks, rabbits, cats, dogs, and bees. The following weekend, she and a local entomologist taught one of the four advanced beekeeping courses per year that they offer – one for each season.

Just as honeybees thrive in a flourishing ecosystem on the farm, Dandelion Springs itself has established a symbiotic role with other entities in its community. The farm recruits interns from Chesterfield Career & Technical Center to help improve farming practices. It hosts participants of all abilities through local nonprofits including Jacob's Chance, Beyond Boundaries, and FreeHorse Arts. Whether the reference point is honeybees or humans, the farm celebrates the interconnectedness of all its creatures. As Conway puts it, "Everything depends on everything."

Address 11011 Beaver Bridge Road, Chesterfield, VA 23838, +1 (804) 404-2388, www.dandelionsprings.com, dandelionspringsapiary@gmail.com | Getting there By car, take VA-76 South to the exit onto SR-288 South, then onto US-360 West, and then turn left onto Winterpock Road to the destination | Hours See website for events schedule | Tip The market where Conway first started selling her Uptown Girls Honey was the Carytown Farmers Market at City Stadium on Sundays from 9am–1pm, May through October (3201 Maplewood Avenue, www.carytownmarket.com).

26 The Egyptian Building
Richmond's temple to medical education

The most iconic building on the campus of the Medical College of Virginia, now affiliated with Virginia Commonwealth University, is the Egyptian Building. Considered one of the finest examples of the Egyptian Revival architecture popularized globally in the early 19th century by Napoleon, the temple-like building is designed to conjure images of Imhotep and the ancient origins of medicine. Until the 1900s, it was the only building on campus, and since its construction in 1844, it has been in continuous use by medical students as a lecture hall, operating theater, and dissecting laboratory. Visitors are welcome to have a look around.

Unlike the temples that inspired it, the Egyptian Building is constructed of brick and cast iron, but with a limestone-colored stucco exterior that would camouflage it well along the banks of the Nile. The five-story building has walls that are narrower at the top than bottom and a façade in *distyle in antis*, featuring winged disks of Horus and columns topped with palm fronds. Much of the interior flourishes, like lotus flowers, scarab beetles, and hieroglyphic inscriptions in praise of gods Aten and Amun, came during the second period of Egyptian revival after Tutankhamun's tomb was discovered in 1922.

The Egyptian Building has its share of macabre lore – the story of Chris Baker in particular. Baker toiled in the basement as custodian of the college's anatomy lab from the 1860s until 1919. Through unofficial duties in that role, Baker became the city's most infamous graverobber. Appreciated by the medical community as a talented anatomist, Baker was also reviled by his own Black community. He was known to troll alms houses for the recently deceased and to snatch freshly interred bodies from the city's cemeteries, particularly those for Black citizens. Local children were warned to stay away from "ole Chris" after dark.

Address 1223 E Marshall Street, Richmond, VA 23298, +1 (804) 782-2777, www.maps.vcu.
edu/mcv/egyptianbldg/index.html | Getting there Bus Pulse to VCU Medical Center
Eastbound Station or bus 1A, 1B, 1C, 7A, 7B, 29X, 56, 64X to Broad & 11th Streets |
Hours Mon–Fri 9am–5pm | Tip To get a feel for the medicine that's been practiced over
the long lifespan of the Egyptian Building, pop over to the VCU campus' Health Sciences
Library, which hosts the Medical Artifacts collection (509 N 12th Street, www.library.vcu.
edu/research-teaching/special-collections-and-archives/collections/medical-artifacts).

27 Evergreen Cemetery
A graveyard abandoned to nature

In the late 19th century, at the height of the Jim Crow era, Richmond's Black and white citizens were segregated in most aspects of life – and also in death. The city's prominent graveyards, like Hollywood and Shockoe, welcomed only white citizens until the 1950s, and out of these exclusionary practices was born Evergreen Cemetery, a burial ground in East Richmond for the city's Black residents.

For several decades, Evergreen was considered one of the premier cemeteries for Black citizens in the South and serves as the final resting place of prominent Richmonders like businesswoman Maggie Walker (1864 – 1943) and editor and activist John Mitchell, Jr. (1863 – 1929). Unfortunately, through mismanagement and a series of ownership changes, all but a small portion of the cemetery has been abandoned since the 1950s. Nature has reclaimed much of the once manicured graveyard.

In the context of the city's historic treatment of its Black citizens, the neglect of Evergreen and its inhabitants is shameful, but the site remains enchanting – a beautiful intertwining of nature and human mortality. The cemetery is a labyrinth of walking paths through acres of forested terrain overtaken by kudzu, periwinkle, and pokeweed. Crooked tombstones are swallowed up by weeds, and obelisks are draped in ivy. Walking through the woods, you will repeatedly think you've reached the edge of the cemetery, only to discover a new set of vine-covered headstones 100 feet further in.

The latest change in ownership occurred in 2022, when the nonprofit Enrichmond, entrusted with preserving Evergreen and several other cultural landmarks, suddenly dissolved, leaving the cemetery orphaned once again. Despite these challenges, a group of volunteers called Friends of East End remains dedicated to its restoration, showing up on weekends to clear out the overgrowth and return dignity to its residents.

Address 50 Evergreen Road, Richmond, VA 23223, www.eastendcemeteryrva.com, friendsofeastend@gmail.com | Getting there Bus 7A, 7B to Nine Mile Road & Echo Avenue | Hours Unrestricted | Tip Pay a visit to Woodland Cemetery, Richmond's second largest burial ground for Black citizens, which is in better shape than Evergreen and the final resting place of tennis star and civil rights activist Arthur Ashe (1943–1993) (2300 Magnolia Road, www.woodlandrestorationfoundation.org).

28 Family Portraits at the Quirk

Legendary characters of Richmond's most fun hotel

According to the gold letters on its large glass windows, the Quirk is a hotel, but it feels more like a contemporary art museum, where you can spend the night. Katie and Ted Ukrop opened the hotel as an offshoot of their art gallery by the same name in a vacant, World War II era department store, which itself became a work of art, a shiny, pink and white gem on the tiara of the Arts District. The space is elegant, vibrant, and, of course, full of quirks.

"We call ourselves a hotel for curious travelers," says Morgan Slade, the hotel's general manager. Piiquing the curiosity of his guests are the *Family Portraits*, a series of paintings strewn throughout the hotel like items in a treasure hunt. When the Ukrops were getting the hotel off the ground, they commissioned artist Sarah Hand to create papier mâché depictions of seven individuals "whose regular presence … inspired the building's character and personality," according to a museum label in the lobby.

Each of the subjects has a backstory, which Katie Ukrop recalls gleefully. Regarding *Nikki*, a UPS delivery driver who befriended hotel staff during near-daily drop-offs, she says, "In reality, she's this very tough woman, but I love how she's made out to look like a Barbie doll." Also featured are ever-present furry friends, *Jane*, *Charlie*, and *Cat Baby*, whose portrait evolved a lore of its own. "Apparently *Cat Baby* was very popular on Grindr in the beginning – 'Meet me by *Cat Baby*,' they'd say," she recalls.

The Quirk brings a light-hearted approach to the city's art scene, and the portraits are emblematic of that attitude. "They help make it a neighborhood hotel, and they're kind of our take on that country-club lineup of presidents when you walk into a fancy place. We're serious about our art," Ukrop says, "but we don't take ourselves too seriously."

Address 201 W Broad Street, Richmond, VA 23220, +1 (804) 340-6040, www.quirkhotels.com | Getting there Bus 3A, 3B, 3C, 14, 50, 78 to Broad & Adams Streets, Pulse to Arts District Westbound Station | Hours Unrestricted during lobby hours | Tip The Arts District comes alive during RVA First Fridays, an art walk sponsored by neighborhood galleries and restaurants on the first Friday of every month. Stop by Black Iris Gallery, an artist-operated social club open to the public during these monthly events (321 W Broad Street, www.blackirissocialclub.com/gallery).

29 _ Fan Guitar and Ukulele

Main Street's little slice of Oahu

Richmond is neither a large city, nor is it a mecca for ukulele enthusiasts, but it nonetheless hosts a shop dedicated almost entirely to that lovely little instrument. Put into context, however, the journey of John and Genie Gonzalez del Solar to the Fan Guitar and Ukulele makes a little more sense.

John studied classical guitar at VCU and then enlisted in the Navy, which led him to Pearl Harbor for four years. "Ukulele was just a part of living in Hawaii and playing music. It's basically a given," he says of his time there. "I had managed a guitar and ukulele store in Hawaii while I was living there, so I had a basic understanding of what it was all about. We opened in 2012, and it was a stressful but magical evolution."

While the store has been present in its current location since it opened, indeed it has evolved. John began manufacturing ukuleles in 2015 and now sells his branded Sparrow ukes at the store. During the Covid-19 lockdown, John says he really leaned into the luthiery side of the business, while the retail side was being devastated. John's best friend Stu Kindle bought half the business and helped the store weather the pandemic, as John puts it, "with his jovial persona and willingness to exaggerate the positive elements of life!" At this point, things are coming up Milhouse, as 2022 was the business's best year ever. And with in-person contact back to baseline, they're expanding ukulele lessons at the shop.

For anyone who can strum a ukulele, which is, well… just about anyone, the store is a joy to walk through, with an inventory to suit all budgets and styles. For the rock fans in the house, there's a wall dedicated to electric ukuleles. If bluegrass is more your jam, a selection of tiny, adorable banjos is available. John, Genie, Stu, and pups Scruffy and Ziggy are usually around to talk shop, spread their wisdom, and share the good vibes.

Address 1215 W Main Street, Richmond, VA 23220, +1 (804) 254-4600, www.uke-fan.com, fanguitarandukulele@gmail.com | Getting there Bus 5, 77, 78 to Main & Harrison Streets | Hours Daily noon–6pm | Tip One of Gonzalez del Solar's favorite places to catch live music is the Tin Pan, a listening room and restaurant that books folk music, jazz, and bluegrass music in an intimate setting (8982 Quioccasin Road, www.tinpanrva.com).

30 _ *Feed Ur Beaver*
Mural, mural on the wall

In 2012, the Richmond Mural Project kicked off an ongoing public art Renaissance in the city. The ingredients had been there all along with a hip counterculture, the country's top-ranked public arts program at VCU, limitless bare brick façades, and the Arts District, which was conspicuously devoid of outdoor art. Since that year, Richmond has welcomed internationally renowned artists to paint more than 150 murals and earned the No. 4 spot on USA Today's Best City for Street Art list in 2023.

The majority of the murals are concentrated in the densely populated neighborhoods of Richmond proper. Many feature highbrow, weighty subjects. Several were painted by career muralists, whose portfolios include the sides of skyscrapers in international capital cities. One notable outlier, a mural entitled *Feed Ur Beaver*, diverges from all of these descriptors, and it's a fan favorite, nonetheless.

In 2015, Alison Miller, the owner of adult novelty shop Taboo, commissioned local tattoo artist Jesse Smith and his colleague Miguel del Cuadro, to paint a mural on the 25 x 75-foot façade of her Midlothian Turnpike location. All three parties swear they intended to create a fun, innocent piece of artwork intentionally devoid of sexuality, so as to avoid controversy. With a bright, cartoonish depiction of a young woman feeding an apple to a woodland creature, it would seem that they accomplished that objective. Not everyone agreed, however.

Some questioned just how young the young woman was, why of all adorable potential apple recipients did the woodland creature have to be a beaver, and would the mural confuse area children into thinking Taboo was actually a bookstore for young readers and unsuspectingly walk in? The flap earned a plaudit from another publication: *Style Weekly*'s coveted award for "Most Overblown Mural Controversy." And the beaver survived to tell the tale.

Address 5100 Midlothian Turnpike, Richmond, VA 23225, +1 (804) 233-4418, www.taboorva.com | Getting there Bus 1A to Midlothian Pike & Covington Road | Hours Unrestricted | Tip A "Fan" favorite among the Richmond Mural Project productions is Etam Cru's *Moonshine*, a rendering of a beautiful woman bathing in a jar of strawberry moonshine, above the parking lot of a 7-Eleven in the Fan neighborhood (1101 W Grace Street).

31 Gardens at Agecroft Hall
A bit of Old Blighty in Windsor Farms

Imagine the year is 1926. You have a tremendous mountain of cash and a beautiful, 23-acre plot of land overlooking the James River. The only thing missing is a house. Why go through the trouble of designing one from scratch when there's a perfectly fine and vacant mansion already sitting there … 3,620 miles across the Atlantic Ocean? Such was the reasoning of Richmond financier T.C. Williams when he made a down payment, sight unseen, on the 15th-century manor house known as Agecroft Hall, located in a suburb of Manchester, England. Williams and his architect Henry G. Morse had the house deconstructed, transported to the US, and rebuilt in Windsor Farms.

The house was a functional home until Williams's widow Elizabeth moved in 1967, and since 1969 it has been a house museum highlighting British lifestyle in the Tudor and Stuart eras. With its architectural flourishes, ornate wooden inlay, ancient furniture, tapestries, stained glass, ancestral portraits, and, most curiously, a mummified cat, the house's every feature, spanning the 12th to 21st centuries, has a story to tell.

Complementing the complex character of the house is an elaborate exterior designed by landscape architect Charles Gillette, whose legacy lives on to this day in backyards and gardens all over Richmond. Gillette arranged the gardens at Agecroft as a series of "rooms," each featuring a different aspect of British horticulture, such as Shakespearean plants or the Elizabethan knot garden. One notable garden contains specimens from the inventory of famed British botanists, the John Tradescants, the younger of whom introduced several native Virginia plants to Great Britain after three visits here in the 1630s. The most iconic feature of the grounds at Agecroft, the "ballroom" if you will, is the rectangular, tiered, sunken garden, which erupts with the vibrancy of 5,300 tulips every spring.

Address 4305 Sulgrave Road, Richmond, VA 23221, +1 (804) 353-4241, www.agecrofthall.org | Getting there Bus 5, 78 to Cary & Nansemond Streets | Hours Tue–Sun noon–5pm | Tip The Virginia House, Agecroft's neighbor to the East, is yet another reconstructed British mansion formerly known as the Priory House, built circa 1566 and rebuilt in 1929. The house is now owned by the Virginia Museum of History and Culture (4301 Sulgrave Road, www.virginiahistory.org/learn/house-tour).

32 Gators at the Jefferson

Pay a visit to the city's snappiest hotel

When David Niven (1910–1983), the British actor who would go on to star in blockbusters of the 1960s like *Pink Panther* and *Casino Royale,* checked into the Jefferson Hotel in 1933 on a road trip to Florida, he was met with something of a shock. He recounted in his memoir *The Moon's a Balloon*: "First stop, Richmond, Virginia, and my eyes now gummed together with tiredness, snapped open with amazement when, just as I was signing the hotel register, I noticed a full sized alligator in a small pool about six feet from the reception desk."

The pool he referenced is one of two fountains in a beautiful atrium known as the Palm Court. The gator was one of a dozen or so who called the hotel home in the first half of the 20th century. One pool held the baby gators, and the other held the adults, at least, that is, until they got curious and wandered off through the lobby.

At the dawn of the motorist era in America, guests traveled back to the Northeast from Florida with baby alligators they had picked up in Florida as souvenirs. Legend has it that they would leave their scaly friends in the fountains once the novelty had worn off. Outside the entrance to the hotel stands a statue of Old Pompey, the last alligator to live at the Jefferson. He died in 1945.

Built in 1895 by cigarette titan Lewis Ginter (1824–1897), the Jefferson Hotel is rife with local lore. The staircase reportedly inspired the grand staircase in *Gone With the Wind.* F. Scott and Zelda Fitzgerald shared the bridal suite here during the height of Prohibition and may have visited the hotel's notorious speakeasy. Comedian Wanda Sykes claims she was haunted by the ghost of an enslaved woman in her room here. In 2018, another predatory, leathery, old reptile was seen marching between the marble columns when the patriarch of HBO's *Succession*, Logan Roy, attended a political conference set inside.

Address 101 W Franklin Street, Richmond, VA 23220, +1 (804) 649-4750, www.jeffersonhotel.com | Getting there Bus 5 to Main & Adams Streets | Hours Lobby unrestricted | Tip The Graduate Hotel, two blocks east of the Jefferson may not have the illustrious history of its neighbor, but it does have the Byrd House, a rooftop bar perched atop 16 stories with one of the best views in Richmond (301 West Franklin Street, www.graduatehotels.com/richmond).

33 Ghost Church
In memory of the pioneers for religious freedom

Freedom of religion is a concept so stitched into the fabric of American life that it's easy to forget the people and events that secured such a guarantee. The Polegreen Church Foundation exists to honor the origins of that right, the people who paved its road to the Constitution, and one very special place in Mechanicsville where they gathered to worship.

The Church of England was the official religion of colonial Virginia, as it was in the majority of the colonies, and the state funded the maintenance of its churches and the salaries of its clergy. Persecution of those practicing other faiths was commonplace. In 1739, a group of Virginians called the Hanover Dissenters broke away from the Church and successfully lobbied the legislature to approve four "reading rooms" across the state, where non-Anglican worship was accepted. One of these was Polegreen Church in Mechanicsville.

Attendees of Polegreen Church, including a young patriot named Patrick Henry (1736 – 1799), advocated for religious toleration in Virginia and ultimately changed the culture of the colony. This evolution culminated in passage of the *Virginia Statute for Religious Freedom*, a precursor to the Establishment Clause of the First Amendment guaranteeing that "Congress shall make no law respecting an establishment of religion."

The church burned down due to gunfire during the Civil War, but in the 1990s, a group funded the excavation of its foundation and the construction of a spectacular monument to religious freedom. The memorial consists of a long brick walkway inlaid with a timeline describing two millennia worth of events in the struggle for religious freedom, leading to a structure of white steel beams colloquially dubbed the "Ghost Church." The memorial reminds visitors that, though the building is gone, its spirit keeps watch over the legacy its adherents fought for nearly three centuries ago.

Address 6411 Heatherwood Drive, Mechanicsville, VA 23116, +1 (804) 730-3837, www.historicpolegreenchurch.org, admin@historicpolegreenchurch.org | Getting there By car, take Mechanicsville Turnpike to I-295 North to exit 38A, turn right onto Pole Green Road then turn left onto Rural Point Road and right onto Heatherwood Drive | Hours Daily dawn–dusk | Tip For more information on religious freedom in Virginia, visit the First Freedom Center, a small museum near the downtown Richmond site where the Virginia Statute for Religious Freedom was signed (14 South 14th Street, www.thevalentine.org/exhibition/first-freedom-center).

34 The Glass Spot

Learn the art of glassmaking from the pros

Water just tastes better when you drink it from a beautiful glass you've personally spun and blown from a blob of molten, orange goo. Master glassmith Chris Skibbe can avail you of that opportunity at the Glass Spot, the Northside studio where he creates museum-quality works and teaches the public how to craft their own, more modest masterpieces.

During the 60–90 minute classes, up to eight students join Skibbe and his assistant to hand-blow a predetermined object, such as drinking glasses, vases, and paperweights, in a style and color of their choosing. Prior to the session, Skibbe sits down with the class to review the equipment and basic principles of glassblowing. Then, one by one, students are invited up to partake in the process.

In the first step, Skibbe's assistant dips the blowpipe, aka the "punty," into a crucible of molten glass inside the first of three furnaces, retrieving at the end a large glob of glowing, oozy, orange glass. He then hands the punty over to the student, who gently rolls the glob into piles of colored glass flecks. From here, the class moves to furnace number 2, a slightly cooler one known industry wide as the "glory hole." Minds out of the gutter, people.

Following its trip into the glory hole, the punty is then set onto a workbench of sorts, where the student blows into it and watches the gelatinous pile of goo blossom into a beautiful glass bubble. Using various medieval, metal implements, Skibbe molds the bubble into a form recognizable as someone's new drinking glass and transfers it to furnace number 3, where it gradually cools down to room temperature in a process called annealing. Twenty-four hours later, metamorphosis complete, the vessel emerges as a glorious goblet. The proud student will spend the whole next day drinking from it, not because they're thirsty, but because they can taste the toil imparted into their cherished chalice, and it's delicious.

Address 2306 N Lombardy Street, Suite A, Richmond, VA 23220, +1 (804) 228-8868, www.richmondglassspot.com, theglassspot@gmail.com | **Getting there** Bus 14 to Brook Road & Lombardy Street | **Hours** See website for schedule | **Tip** Located just next door to the Glass Spot is a cool and unusual store called Crewel and Unusual, which creates custom embroidery. The shop is also a studio, and customers can peek into the area where stylish custom patches are made (2306 N Lombardy Street, crewelandunusual.com).

35 Goochland Drive-In
A double-feature dose of nostalgia

There are approximately 300 drive-in theaters operating in the US, down from a peak of more than 4,000 in the late 1950s. With the advent of the VCR, the drive-in nearly went extinct, but a wave of family-friendly nostalgia in the past couple of decades has kept the industry alive. The format was especially appreciated during the COVID-19 lockdowns, when drive-in theaters generated an estimated 90% of total theater revenue nationwide.

Thanks to the Goochland Drive-In, Richmonders are among the lucky Americans with access to the silver screen from the comfort of their cars. Since 2009, the theater has married its retro vibe to state-of-the-art equipment beaming crisp images onto two 40-foot-wide screens and crystal clear audio via FM radio. On most weekends from March to November, the theater welcomes up to 350 cars to view a new release double feature. The opening film starts at dusk, but families are encouraged to arrive at 6:00pm, get settled, and enjoy the cornhole courts and playground while awaiting showtime.

As far as cinematic fare goes, those delightful "Let's All Go to the Lobby" classics gleefully marching on screen are available, as are standard retro-diner classics like burgers and hot dogs, alongside contemporary fare, like the BeyondBurger. During the summer months, the ice cream bar opens up and offers moviegoers soft serve, floats, and sundaes.

There are many ways to get situated at the theater. The straight-laced spectator may simply sit facing forward as they would when driving. Outdoorsy types may want to set up some folding chairs around the car. The preferred method, though, is to stack a mountain of pillows and blankets into your truck bed or trunk and get snug under the stars in the cool, Goochland night air. The next time the modern world has got you down, pile the kids into the station wagon and warp time with a visit to the Goochland Drive-in.

Address 4344 Old Fredericksburg Road, Hadensville, VA 23067, www.goochlanddriveintheater.com, info@goochlanddriveintheater.com | Getting there By car, take I-95 North to exit 64 onto I-64 West, then take exit 153 and turn left onto Old Fredericksburg Road to the destination | Hours See website for showtimes | Tip For another vintage cinematic experience, visit the Henrico Theater, a 1936 movie palace. Not immune to inflation, the Henrico Theater has raised ticket prices from 25 cents all the way to $1 (305 E Nine Mile Road, Henrico, www.henrico.us/rec/places/henrico-theatre).

36 _ Governor's Antiques

A maze of architectural treasure

Governor's Architectural Antiques is so huge that, upon arrival, visitors are handed a treasure map of sorts, loosely identifying where the store's five million pieces of treasure are kept within a labyrinth spread over seven acres and 45,000 feet of interior space. The tour begins in the massive, indoor salvage room, a collection of items so grand and peculiar – an old elevator car, a revolving door apparatus, a cigarette machine, a German light bulb tester – that it's hard to imagine where these objects could possibly end up in this day and age. Wind through row after row of showcases in the adjacent rooms, dedicated to the more refined, curated, smaller items, like piles of Victorian hardware, vintage advertising ephemera, military collectibles, and stained glass.

After the hardware room, head over to "The Bottom," another warehouse of salvaged goods needing repair, enclosed by the workshops, where a stable of master craftsmen rebuild furniture, rewire light fixtures, cut antique glass, weld iron fencing, and more. From there, get your steps in perusing the outdoor holdings, including 450 clawfoot tubs, 20 different styles of antique, municipal lamp posts, over a mile of wrought iron gates, and 19 shipping containers, each with a different category of artifact. "Don't miss container number 13," the lady at the front desk advises. "That one's for mannequins and pool tables."

As with each piece of its treasure, Governor's has been on a journey of its own over the past 50 years. Founded in 1970 by Gary Thomas, the store was more of a traditional antique collection for the first few decades but shifted focus to architectural and industrial salvage when Thomas' son Jeff took over. The inventory has grown exponentially, and so too has its organization. Whether you're renovating a Victorian mansion or just love cool, old stuff, you're in for an epic treasure hunt.

Address 8000 Antique Lane, Mechanicsville, VA 23116, +1 (804) 746-1030, www.governorsantiques.com, info@governorsantiques.com | Getting there By car, take the Mechanicsville Turnpike east to I-295 then north to the Pole Green Road. Drive east, turn left onto Antique Lane, and continue to the destination | Hours Tue–Sat, 9am–5pm | Tip On the other end of the size spectrum from Governor's, Tiny Space is a diminutive second-hand store in Church Hill. Though the space limits the inventory, the expertly curated items turn over quickly, so no two visits are alike (2708 E Marshall Street, www.instagram.com/tinyspace.rva).

37 Grant's HQ from *Lincoln*

Hollywood finds history in Petersburg

Steven Spielberg's Oscar-winning biopic *Lincoln* portrays the 16th president's dogged pursuit of the amendment to abolish slavery. Spoiler alert: the 13th Amendment passed, though by a razor-thin, two-vote margin. At the height of the suspenseful roll call in the House chamber, the scene cuts to Union soldiers nervously keeping count as each vote is buzzed in via telegraph to the headquarters of General Ulysses S. Grant.

This scene was shot in a magnificent octagonal brick building in the center of Old Towne Petersburg called City Market. Constructed in 1878, the building was a meat and produce market until the late 20th century, and it now hosts Croaker's Spot, one of Richmond's hallowed providers of soul food. The building has been featured in other period pieces, like *Mercy Street* and *Turn*.

Grant's actual headquarters in the final months of the war were at City Point, about 10 miles northeast of the film set, and one of the original wooden structures where he operated is still standing. The film features several scenes set in these buildings and aboard the boat *River Queen* anchored there, where Lincoln spent two of the last three weeks of his life planning the end of the war with Grant.

Lincoln, which was filmed entirely in Virginia, features other prominent buildings in Petersburg. James Spader's character William N. Bilbo (c. 1822–1867) narrowly avoids a gunfight outside the Brickhouse Run restaurant. Lincoln gives a speech outside Union Station and later has a heartfelt discussion with a congressman outside the historic McIlwaine House. Secretary of State William Seward (1801–1972) is shown having beers and crabs at the Appomattox Iron Works. On shooting the film where these pivotal events had occurred Spielberg said in a 10Mile SceneCine video, "There was … a nice feeling of healing to be able to tell the story at the heart of the former Confederacy."

Address 9 E Old Street, Petersburg, VA 23803, +1 (804) 957-5635, www.croakersspot.com |
Getting there By car, take I-95 South to exit 53, turn right onto E Washington Street,
right onto N Adams Street, left onto Bollingbrook Street, right onto Cockade Alley, and
left onto E Old Street | Hours Mon–Thu 11am–9pm, Fri 11am–10pm, Sat noon–10pm,
Sun noon–9pm | Tip For a peek at the lifestyle in antebellum Virginia, visit Centre Hill
Mansion, "Petersburg's most stately home." The museum here hosted an exhibit dedicated
to the costumes of *Lincoln* after the release of the film (1 Centre Hill Court, Petersburg,
www.historicpetersburg.org/centre-hill-mansion).

38 — Grave of Lady Wonder

Pay tribute to the Mare of Richmond

Founded in 1929 by a local veterinarian and still in operation to this day, Pet Memorial Park is an animal cemetery that serves as the final resting place to more than 4,000 of Richmond's feathered and furry friends. Although flashbacks of Stephen King's *Pet Sematary* are inevitable during a visit here, perusing the headstones dating back to the 1920s is endlessly fascinating. The majority of its inhabitants are dogs and cats, but you'll also find ducks, rabbits, a goat, a chimpanzee, and of course, a famous psychic horse.

In 1926, a Richmond woman named Claudia Fonda began to notice something special about her horse that she had purchased the previous year, a two-year-old filly named Lady. With a mere unspoken wish, Lady would appear by her side. Sensing that the horse had more to say, Mrs. Fonda taught her the alphabet and fashioned a giant typewriter contraption, with which Lady could reportedly spell out messages. Before long, word spread of the horse's talents, not only mere mortal skills like spelling and arithmetic, but of supernatural gifts like mind-reading and clairvoyance, earning her the more fitting title of 'Lady Wonder.'

The Fondas began scheduling meetings for visitors, each paying 50 cents to ask three questions of the horse. An estimated 150,000 people visited Lady Wonder at her stable in Chesterfield County for counsel. She became famous for her soothsaying, including accurate predictions of 14 out of 17 World Series champions and all but one presidential election in her lifetime (she whiffed on the Dewey-Truman matchup, though she was hardly alone there). So revered were her talents that investigators from four separate missing children cases across the country came to Virginia seeking her help. In March 1957, at the age of 33, Lady Wonder died from a heart attack and was laid to rest at Pet Memorial Park before an adoring crowd.

Address 1697 Terrell Drive, Richmond, VA 23229, +1 (804) 639-4591,
www.facebook.com/petmemorialparks, petmemorialparks@gmail.com | Getting there
Bus 79 to Three Chopt Road & Westbury Drive | Hours Daily 8am–5pm | Tip Another
iconic Richmond horse is *War Horse*, the sculpture by Tessa Pullan, which can be found
on the steps of the Virginia Museum of History & Culture. The downtrodden stallion is a
monument to the estimated 1.5 million horses who were wounded or killed during the Civil
War (428 N Arthur Ashe Boulevard, www.virginiahistory.org).

39___ GWARbar

Where death metal meets fine dining

Most restaurateurs would be devastated to hear their establishments described as "disgusting" or "revolting," but for GWARbar's executive chef BalSac the Jaws o' Death, aka Michael Derks, those adjectives fit the brand he and his bandmates have diligently cultivated over the past few decades. Sure, GWARbar serves delicious pub fare, but with blood-spattered walls and the detached limbs of fake intergalactic creatures hanging from the ceiling, there's still plenty to unsettle you while you enjoy your food.

Situated in the Jackson Ward neighborhood, just two blocks from where death metal band GWAR formed in 1985, GWARbar is a culinary homage to Richmond's most polarizing band. In the band's early days, metalheads the universe over ate up the vile slurry of sex, violence, and clangor served at their legendary concerts. The conservative stewards of polite society that controlled local government in the 1990s, however, did not and had the hometown antiheroes banned from playing here for a period. Although just one piece of a fierce counter culture in Richmond, GWAR must be credited with pushing the boundaries into a new dimension.

BalSac still tours with GWAR but also serves up slightly more traditional dishes these days. The mainstay of their menu has to be the pulled pork on a brioche bun dubbed simply "Meat Sandwich," sharing its name with the band's 1995 metal ballad. For a namesake so focused on death and destruction though, GWARbar has a surprisingly robust, meat-free menu, with offerings like a vegan barbecue dish called the "Hail Seitan" and a veggie burger dubbed the "We Don't Kill Everything," a nuanced reference to GWAR's 1999 album, *We Kill Everything*.

The next time you crave a side of food with your death metal, grab a late-night bite at GWARbar and, to quote the Scumdogs of the Universe, "eat it, scarf it, bite it, cram it, down it, chow it, want it, pig out!"

Address 217 W Clay Street, Richmond, VA 23220, +1 (804) 918-9352, www.gwarbar.com, contact@gwarbar.com | Getting there Bus 3A, 3B, 3C, 14, 50, 78 to Broad & Adams Streets | Hours Daily 4pm–2am | Tip Richmond has nurtured a healthy heavy-metal scene, and though many of the city's best metal venues have come and gone, Wonderland remains a stalwart. A menagerie of creepy neon clowns in the rafters set the appropriate tone for headbangers to mosh (1727 E Main Street, www.facebook.com/wonderland-rva).

40 Hall of Presidents

An ode to the Mother of Presidents

Virginians are very proud that their state has sent a record eight of its citizens to the American presidency, and nowhere does the proverbial back-patting reverberate louder than the Hall of Presidents at the Virginia Statehouse. A magnificent three-story chamber capped by a 30-foot rotunda, the room commands solemnity for its marble inhabitants: busts of Jefferson, Madison, Monroe, Taylor, Tyler, Harrison, Wilson, the Marquis de Lafayette (historical tidbit, NOT an American president), and standing centerstage, a magnificent statue of the granddaddy of them all, George Washington.

The statue of Washington is notable for reportedly having the most accurate likeness of the man. The sculpture was completed by Jean-Antoine Houdon, a noted French sculptor, who spent two weeks at Mount Vernon measuring the former President and smearing oil on his face to cast a plaster mask. When Houdon finished the statue, the Statehouse had not yet been completed, and it was instead displayed in the Louvre for several years. It was finally installed at the Statehouse on May 14, 1796 and has stood on display in the exact same spot ever since.

Emanating from the atrium are several rooms where some of the most important events in American history have played out. To the north stands the Old Hall of the House of Delegates, where the US Bill of Rights was ratified, Aaron Burr was tried, and Robert E. Lee became commander of the Confederate army. To the east and west respectively, stand the House and Senate chambers, where the oldest governing body in the Americas, the Virginia House of Delegates, continues to legislate. The House chamber served as the set for the climax of Steven Spielberg's Oscar-winning film *Lincoln*, in which the amendment abolishing slavery was passed, ironically adjacent to the actual room where Virginia lawmakers voted to secede from the Union.

Address 1000 Bank Street, Richmond, VA 23218, +1 (804) 698-1788, www.virginiacapitol.gov, capitoltourguides@house.virginia.gov | Getting there Bus 2A, 2B, 2C, 5, 64X to 9th & Main Streets | Hours Mon–Sat 9am–5pm, Sun 1–5pm | Tip Also featured in *Lincoln* is the Virginia Governor's mansion, located around the corner from the Statehouse. Built in 1813, the Governor's mansion is the oldest in the nation still in use (1111 Capitol Street, www.executivemansion.virginia.gov).

41 Hanover Tavern
America's first dinner theater

If you find yourself at the Hanover Theater to catch a musical, also take a moment to appreciate just how much has happened here. Before he was prattling on about liberty and death, Patrick Henry (1736–1799) tended bar and fiddled for patrons there. The inn hosted both Lord Cornwallis (aka the leader of the Brits) and Generals Washington and Lafayette (aka the leaders of the Yanks) during the Revolutionary War. Eight decades later, the tavern welcomed Union and Confederate troops alike en route to combat. Edgar Allan Poe, Charles Dickens, and PT Barnum are among the cultural icons who spent the night there.

Despite its epic history, by the 1950s, the tavern was abandoned and had fallen into disrepair, but it was saved by an unlikely crew. According to a plaque on the wall, "[o]n August 1, 1953, six actors, two children, a dog, a cat, and two pigs moved in… determined to make it their personal home and a professional theatre… and they did." Calling themselves the Barksdale Theatre, the troupe lived upstairs and put on plays downstairs, all the while making crucial renovations to the dilapidated space, which, per another placard on site, had "no heat in the building, no working plumbing, crumbling walls, and a littered badland of a backyard."

Beyond rescuing the landmark, the group made history of its own. Acting on feedback from their hungry audience members, the crew began providing food to the guests while they watched the plays. Eventually, the room adjacent to the stage became a proper buffet, thus creating the nation's first dinner theater. The Barksdale Theatre was also the first performing arts group in Virginia to integrate their audiences and cast, defying Jim Crow-era laws and norms of the time. In 2012, the group morphed into the Virginia Repertory Theatre, which carries on the legacy of the Barksdale players in the space they rebuilt.

Address 13181 Hanover Courthouse Road, Hanover, VA 23069, +1 (804) 537-5050, www.hanovertavern.org | Getting there By car, follow I-95 North to exit 92A onto SR-54 East and then turn right onto Hanover Courthouse Road | Hours Wed – Sat 11am – 8pm, Sun 11am – 7pm | Tip The Swift Creek Mill Theatre is another historic performing arts group in South Chesterfield. The old mill in which shows are performed dates to around 1850 (17401 Jefferson Davis Highway, South Chesterfield, www.swiftcreekmill.com).

42 Henry "Box" Brown Memorial

Memorial to a daring escape from enslavement

In downtown Richmond is a sculpture in the shape of a box. You could easily mistake it for a municipal trash can or mailbox. It actually commemorates one of the most innovative legends in Richmond history. It's a quirky story, though one arising from tragic circumstances.

Henry Brown was born enslaved at Hermitage Plantation in Louisa County. At the age of 15, enslavers took him from his parents and forced him to work in a tobacco warehouse in downtown Richmond. Later, his pregnant wife and three young children were auctioned off to a plantation in North Carolina. He never saw them again.

Heartbroken, Brown began to plot his escape from slavery. He enlisted two friends to help him build a wooden crate, 3 feet wide, 2.5 feet tall, and 2 feet deep – just large enough for him to fit inside. On March 29, 1859, Brown stamped the words "DRY GOODS" on the side, climbed inside, and had his friends ship the box from Richmond, VA to Philadelphia, PA.

The journey was not easy. Despite a warning stamped on the top of the crate, "This Side Up With Care," the box was upside-down for a good portion of the trip. After 27 hours aboard boats, trains, and wagons, the box arrived in Philadelphia. The recipients of the box pried the top off, and Brown sprang out reportedly exclaiming, "How do you do, gentlemen?" Hence, the word "Box" in his name. He went on to advocate for abolition, first in the Northeast and then in England, where he moved to avoid the Fugitive Slave Act of 1850.

This seemingly simple memorial gives a sense of how uncomfortable Brown must have been during his journey and the bleak conditions that made the gamble worth it. A quote from Brown inscribed on the memorial reads, "Buoyed by the prospect of Freedom... I was willing to dare even death itself."

Address 1498 Dock Street, Richmond, VA 23219, www.slaverymonuments.org/items/ show/1217 | Getting there Bus 1A, 1B, 1C to 14th & Dock Streets | Hours Unrestricted | Tip Not far from Henry "Box" Brown Plaza, at the site of a former auction house, is the Richmond Slavery Reconciliation Statue, a memorial acknowledging the city's role in the trade of enslaved people. Identical statues exist in Liverpool, England and Cotonou, Benin to form a triangle commemorating the beginning, middle, and end of their tragic journey (15th & East Main Streets, www.broadbent.studio/reconciliation-triangle).

43 Hollywood Rapid

The best urban whitewater in the country

It's no coincidence that Richmond has rapids running through its downtown. When John Smith and Christopher Newport tried to sail up the James in 1607 in search of the Northwest Passage, the rocks at the Fall Line stopped them dead in their tracks. As Smith wrote in his book, *A True Relation of Virginia,* "We were intercepted with great craggy stones in the midst of the river where the water falleth so rudely, and with such a violence, as not any boat can possibly passe…." Smith and his delicate sensibilities may not have appreciated the rapids, but it is that very whitewater that draws adrenaline junkies to Richmond.

Contrary to Smith's account, boats do, in fact, navigate the Fall Line rapids, though headed in the opposite direction. Since the opening of breaks in the Belle Isle dam in the 1970s, whitewater enthusiasts have paddled kayaks, canoes, and inflatable rafts down the Lower James between the put-in at Reedy Creek and the take-out at the 14th Street Bridge. These used to be the only class IV rapids within American city limits, but the un-damming of the Chattahoochee River in March 2012 allowed Columbus, Georgia to share the claim.

The most iconic rapid on the Lower James is Hollywood, named for the cemetery ominously overlooking it. To onlookers on the shore of Belle Isle, just a few feet from the Hollywood drop, experienced boaters make the rapid look easy, but the class III-IV rapid can be treacherous. The entrance to Hollywood lies between two holes named Stripper and Flipper, Richmond's own Scylla and Charybdis. The current then funnels into the Hollywood drop, looking like a smooth shard of dragonglass jutting into a cauldron of whitewater, including a notorious boat-swallowing hole called the Washing Machine. Book your adventure with Riverside Outfitters, whose seasoned guides have been shepherding people through these rapids since 2005.

Address 1 Belle Isle, Richmond, VA 23225, +1 (804) 560-0068, www.riversideoutfitters.com | Getting there Bus 87 to 2nd Street & Brown's Island Way | Hours Viewable daily dawn–dusk from Bell Isle; see website for whitewater trips | Tip The Youell Bridge in Maidens is a low, single-lane bridge providing a unique view of a tranquil stretch of the James. To get there, drive around the abandoned 19th-century prison building off River Road (1900 River Road W, Crozier).

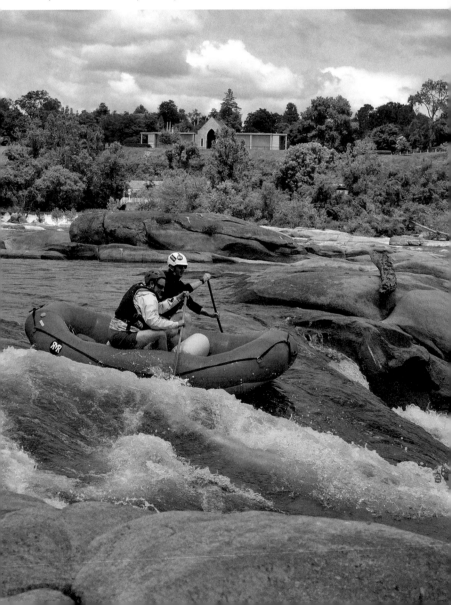

44 Hotel Greene

Mystery, intrigue, and miniature golf

Entering Hotel Greene feels like the opening of a novel *in media res*. Important things have happened here, but what? There are hints of grandeur and hints of decay. Persian rugs and chandeliers exist alongside peeling wallpaper and exposed pipes. What decade is it? Is this purgatory? Is David Lynch involved here? There are so many unanswered questions that you just decide to stop thinking and putt.

Let's start with what we know to be true. Hotel Greene is a miniature golf course set inside a fake grand hotel built into the ruins of an actual grand hotel. The real one was the Hotel John Marshall, which was at one point the largest in Virginia and the focal point of high society in Richmond. Built in 1929, the John Marshall's 16 stories loomed over downtown, and her 418 rooms hosted several US presidents and Winston Churchill. Unfortunately, the hotel could not keep up with the evolution of the industry and was converted into condos in 2008, leaving the building with a lot of empty hospitality space … space perfect for a miniature golf course with a cryptic storyline.

Which brings you back to mysterious goings-on in a nebulous time and locale. From the first tee, you weave your way from the lobby into the spa, through hallways, bedrooms, and bathrooms, all the while picking up clues about an opaque story, where you're not sure if you're an observer, a guest, or a ghost. The lighting is dim. Phones ring ominously. While you figure all of this out, you try desperately not to six-putt.

The experience culminates in the all-in final putt into Hellmouth, a vertigo-inducing, steep, narrow ramp into the mouth of a demon. If you nail the putt, you win a t-shirt not otherwise sold. Alas, you miss the Hellmouth putt, but you will return for another crack at it, and for the excellent cocktails – and also to figure out what the hell is the meaning of all of this.

Address 508 E Franklin Street, Richmond, VA 23219, +1 (804) 447-5958, www.hotelgreene.com, info@hotelgreene.com | Getting there Bus 5, 14 to Main & S 5th Streets | Hours Wed 5–11pm, Thu 2–11pm, Fri 5pm–midnight, Sat 10am–midnight, Sun 10am–6pm | Tip Another accommodation teeming with local lore is the Linden Row Inn, just a few blocks west of Hotel Greene. Enjoy drinks in the "enchanted garden," where Edgar Allan Poe played as a boy and courted his first sweetheart Elmira Royster (100 E Franklin Street, www.lindenrowinn.com).

45 Iron Dog

Steadfast guardian of Hollywood Cemetery

With nuances both beautiful and bizarre, steeped in history and nature, built by enslaved laborers but honoring mainly Confederates and prominent White Richmonders, Hollywood Cemetery encapsulates the soul of Richmond in ways good and bad. Defying stereotypes of graveyards, Hollywood is bright and leafy, and on an ordinary day, you will pass the likes of joggers, mothers pushing strollers, and tourists on Segways enjoying some of the city's most beautiful vistas. Even four-legged friends on leashes are welcome and may stop short at the sight of the Iron Dog, a cast-iron statue of a large Newfoundland standing over the small, cradle-shaped grave of Florence Bernardin Rees, who died at age two of scarlet fever on February 7, 1862.

Many stories of how the Iron Dog came to look over Florence abound, but consensus seems to support the following narrative. Cast by a Baltimore foundry in the 1850s, the statue was a fixture in front of the photography gallery located at 145 Main Street belonging to Florence's uncle, Charles Rees. While alive, Florence loved the statue, and when she and her father visited the studio, she could be found out front petting and hugging it.

When Florence died, Charles gifted the statue to her parents, who kept it for a while at their home. At some point during the war, the Confederate government began appropriating whatever decorative iron it could find to melt into munitions at Tredegar Ironworks. Presuming that the collectors would spare cemetery memorials, the Rees family moved the statue to Florence's gravesite, and there it has stood ever since.

These days, people pay tribute to Florence and the dog in the form of bows, bandanas, treats, toys, jewelry, and other gifts. Imaginative visitors have also claimed to hear growling near the grave and report seeing the silhouette of a dog and a little girl strolling in the moonlight.

Address 412 S Cherry Street, Richmond, VA 23220, +1 (804) 648-8501, www.hollywoodcemetery.org | Getting there Bus 3A, 3B, 3C to Spring & Belvidere Streets | Hours See website for seasonal hours | Tip Living, breathing canines will enjoy the fresh air at Barker Field, the city's largest dog park, located at Byrd Park, not too far from Hollywood (1300 Blanton Avenue).

46 Ironclad Coffee

A great cuppa joe and the city's oldest can

The space inside Ironclad Coffee is so beautiful, and the brews are so delicious that it feels wrong to reduce the shop to the rusty old commode sitting in the alley out back, but such is life when your establishment hosts its city's oldest flushing toilet. Constructed in 1884, the building was originally a fire station used by the No. 2 Hook and Ladder Company, so it's likely that one of the city's early firemen christened Richmond's pioneering potty.

The toilet obviously steals the show, but Ironclad has a few other things going for it. Owner Ryan O'Rourke moved his fledgling roastery into the space in 2018 and got to work adding modern amenities and Richmond-centric decor over 19th-century beams and exposed brick. One notable addition is another special old seat - the original shoeshine setup from the Jefferson Hotel that was reportedly used by FDR, Harry Truman, Frank Sinatra, Charlie Chaplin, and Elvis Presley. The shop offers shoeshines Friday–Sunday, which come with a free cup of coffee.

On that topic, Ironclad brews some of the River City's finest joe. They offer rotating single-origin brews and a series of Richmond-inspired blends, such as the Poe-themed "House of Usher" or the "Bare-knuckle Espresso," honoring a man named Tom Molineaux, who literally boxed his way out of enslavement on a Virginia plantation in the early 1800s.

While supplying Richmonders with their morning fix, the shop is also fixing up the city's landscape. In 2022, O'Rourke advocated for the conversion of the rundown lot adjacent to the shop into "Ironclad National Park," an urban oasis with newly installed concrete benches and flora native to Virginia. So next time you're downtown in need of caffeine, grab a cup of Ironclad, and saddle up on your seat of choice, be it a scenic park bench, a handsome wooden stool, or, ideally, the original throne of our firefighting forefathers.

Address 1805 E Grace Street, Richmond, VA 23223, +1 (804) 709-0998, www.ironcladcoffee.com, info@ironcladcoffee.com | **Getting there** Bus 7A, 7B, 56 to Broad & 18th Streets | **Hours** Mon–Fri 7am–5pm, Sat & Sun 8am–5pm | **Tip** Another decommissioned firehouse just up the road from Ironclad once hosted Engine Company 2 and is now home to an excellent burger joint, Station 2 (2016 E Main Street, www.station2richmond.com).

47 Jewish-American Hall of Fame

A Shockoe celebration of Jewish accomplishment

Richmond might not seem like the most obvious choice for host of the Jewish-American Hall of Fame (JAHF), but it is … sort of. While the JAHF itself is headquartered in New York, as a division of the American Jewish Historical Society, the awards presented annually in honor of new inductees are on permanent display at the Virginia Holocaust Museum. The JAHF honors new members each year with an ornate, trapezoidal bronze plaque about the size of a dinner plate, featuring their visage on one side and a depiction of their accomplishments on the other. Across 55 years, the JAHF has honored 63 individuals and one institution, the Touro Synagogue.

At the entrance of the museum, you will walk by an authentic Deutsche Reichsbahn cattle car and past cobblestones collected from the streets of the Warsaw ghetto and now held in place by sections of the railroad track that once led into the Treblinka extermination camp in Poland. The doors open into an enormous, dark, peaceful space. The room is a reconstruction of the choral synagogue from Kovno, Lithuania, site of the ghetto from which the museum's founder Jay Ipson and his family escaped Nazi control. To the right, look for a replica of the Kovno ark, considered one of the finest in the world, and across the pews, lined up neatly are the 55 JAHF plaques.

These glistening relics celebrating Jewish achievement provide an emotional contrast against the somber subject matter elsewhere within its walls, and the museum ties the two together poignantly with this statement: "[a]s people gaze on the portraits of Albert Einstein, George Gershwin, Ruth Bader Ginsburg, Joseph Pulitzer, Dr. Jonas Salk, et al, it is hoped that visitors will reflect on what contributions to humanity might have been made by the six million Jews (and their descendants) whose lives were viciously taken in the Holocaust."

Justice, Justice Shall You Pursue

A fundamental concept to Jewish life is the notion of doing deeds of justice, charitable actions to assist any person in deed. That principle emerges as a cornerstone to all Western thought and belief. It loomed as a dominant theme in the religious and Enlightenment philosophies that guided the hearts and minds of the "founding fathers and mothers" of the American Republic. Jewish-American women and men practiced that ideal believing they needed to return something to the United States for the blessings of liberty and freedom the nation accorded them. From the early years of the Republic, the Deuteronomical command to do justly, to behave charitably for the general welfare of all became a Jewish hallmark be it in providing benevolent social services, engaging in medical and scientific research or seeking to ameliorate the lives of all Americans through legal and judicial reforms.

Rebecca Gratz (1781–1869)

When just 21 years of age, Rebecca Gratz became secretary of the Female Association for the Relief of Women and Children in Reduced Circumstances and in 1819 founded the Philadelphia Orphan Society. Daughter of influential Philadelphia Jewish society, she had learned the value of assisting others in her childhood. Though she would never marry, she provided a home for her orphaned brothers and cared for her sister Rachel when she provided a home for her orphaned of her more significant accomplishments was the creation of the Hebrew Sunday School Society, the first of its kind in America and the model for Jewish education in America. Hearing of her charm, beauty and kindness, Sir Walter Scott based the character "Rebecca" in his classic novel *Ivanhoe* on her. With reference to that rare woman, the British author George Eliot noted, "were all virtue and religion dead, she would make them nearly, being what she was."

Sculpted by Carla Diez Weiner, 1981

Samuel Gompers (1850–1924) and Sidney Hillman (1887–1946)

Gompers and Hillman shaped American labor unions and organized for workers' rights. Samuel Gompers arrived in New York from London at 13. Within a year, he joined the Cigar Makers International Union... scholarship, the American Federation of Labor. Sidney Hillman, a rabbinical student from Lithuania, landed in America in 1907 and found work in a Chicago garment factory. He quickly became a union organizer. In 1915 Hillman founded the Congress of Industrial Organizations. Friedrich Franklin helped to pass the passage of the Hillman, more than any other man, helped to pass the passage of the minimum wage law of 1938.

Justice Ruth Bader Ginsburg (b.1933)

When Ruth Bader Ginsburg was appointed by President Bill Clinton and sworn in as the 107th justice to the United States Supreme Court on August 10, 1993, she became the second woman justice (Sandra Day O'Connor was the first) and the first Jewish woman ever to sit on the Court. After celebrating her eightieth birthday, Justice Ginsburg indicated that she had no plan to retire, saying "I will stay in this job as long as I can do it full steam." Prompted by her own experiences, Ginsburg established the ACLU Women's Rights Project in 1972 so that "artificial barriers are removed, and avenues of opportunity [are] held open to women." The National Women's Hall of Fame sums up Ginsburg's service on the Supreme Court as: "Justice Bader Ginsburg has become known for her scholarly, balanced opinions and forthright personal courage. A cancer survivor herself, she has assisted thousands by her example of frank discussion of the state of her health and early diagnosis."

Ernestine Rose (1810–1892)

Daughter of a rabbi, Ernestine Louise Potowski was born in Piotrkov, Poland. Rejecting an arranged marriage at the age of 16, she singularly made her way to America via Germany and Britain, where she married William Rose. Speaking out against slavery in South Carolina in 1847, she was threatened with being tarred and feathered. Those threats did not impede her opposition to... and weighty social issues. She petitioned the New York State Assembly to pass the Married Women's Property bill that permitted women to control their own assets after marriage. At the first Woman's Rights Convention (1850), she noted: "We have heard a...

Louis D. Brandeis (1856–1941)

Brandeis's elevation on the first Jewish justice on the Supreme Court aroused considerable consternation in many circles when he was nominated by President Woodrow Wilson in 1916. Labeled as the Wall Street Journal as a "radical... super-solvent... anti-corporation agitator," Brandeis was nevertheless confirmed. Even before assuming his seat on the Supreme Court, Brandeis made it clear that "America's fundamental law seeks to make real the brotherhood of man's democracy..." To the American enemy is the social justice... Throughout his life, he counseled on behalf of ordinary working people, spoke out for research rights and argued against colonial corporate monopolies. He likewise... Working with President Wilson and other...

Herbert H. Lehman (1878–1963)

...

Address 2000 E Cary Street, Richmond, VA 23223, +1 (804) 257-5400, www.vaholocaust.org | **Getting there** Bus 14 to Main & 21st Streets | **Hours** Mon–Fri 9am–5pm, Sat & Sun 11am–5pm | **Tip** Congregation Beth Ahabah in the Fan is descended from the first synagogue in Richmond that was founded in 1789. The sanctuary displays 29 beautiful, stained glass windows, including one by Louis Comfort Tiffany, and operates a museum dedicated to the Jewish experience in Richmond (1121 W Franklin Street, www.bethahabah.org).

48 John Marshall Barber Shop
Historic handlers of high-profile hair

The professionals at the John Marshall Barber Shop are the unofficial caretakers of Virginia's most prominent coifs. Set in the lobby of the former Hotel John Marshall, Richmond's oldest barber shop opened its doors on October 29, 1929, a date better known in American history as Black Tuesday, when the stock market crashed. Despite the ominous beginning, the nearly 100-year-old shop survived the Great Depression and the closure of its namesake hotel with a steady stream of customers flowing down from Capitol Square.

The shop has maintained its floors, walls, and mirrors, and if they could talk, they'd have stories to tell about the mile-long list of politicians, dignitaries, and celebrities who have received a trim here. Fortunately, another fixture, somewhat younger and certainly more loquacious, is there to regale customers with those tales: the gentlemanly owner Hugh Campbell, who started as an apprentice in 1968 and eventually bought the shop in 1989.

"There's Elvis leaving the shop," he says, pointing to a photo of a heavy-set King, full-faced and replete with nicely trimmed sideburns. "And there I am finishing up with the older Bush... but W was in here too, y'know." According to a placard put up by the shop's former owner, so too were some 63 other famous individuals, including several other presidents (FDR, JFK, Ford, Carter), Winston Churchill, Fats Domino, Gary Cooper, John Wayne, Martin Luther King, Jr., Redd Foxx, Alex Trebek, and Bruce Willis. Lining the walls are the autographed headshots of famous Virginia politicians, including every governor since the 1950s, most of them thanking Campbell for the tight cut.

Campbell is rightfully proud of his shop, but he also enjoys giving it a gentle poke in the ribs from time to time, as he does with his regulars. As a customer checks out, Campbell says with a wink, "Glad you could make it into the bottom of the John."

Address 502 E Franklin Street, Richmond, VA 23219, +1 (804) 649-7577 | Getting there Bus 14 to 5th & Grace Streets | Hours Mon–Fri 8am–6pm, Sat 8am–2pm | Tip After your trim, swing around the block to Rappahannock Oyster Company for some Olde Salts and a crabcake, which *Food & Wine* named the nation's best - sorry, Baltimore (320 E Grace Street, www.rroysters.com/rappahannock-richmond-va.html).

49 John Marshall's Wine Cellar

Keeper of supreme libations

John Marshall (1755–1835) is the longest serving Chief Justice in the history of the Supreme Court and undoubtedly the individual who most defined the culture of its justices. Over his 35-year tenure, Marshall elevated the role of the judiciary from a lesser branch to a full partner with sole discretion to interpret the meaning of the Constitution. He also built a culture of cohesion among the justices, which he accomplished with the help of his preferred potent potable, Madeira wine. The Chief Justice kept a supply of the wine in the cellar at his home in downtown Richmond.

Marshall built his house at the corner of 9th and what is now called Marshall Street, where he, his family, and enslaved servants lived from 1790 to 1835, a period that spanned his tenure as a Congressman, Secretary of State, and Chief Justice. Every February, Marshall made the trek to Washington for the annual Supreme Court session and likely brought along some bottles of Madeira.

The justices convened in DC for just two months of the year to hear and rule on all the cases for that session. Marshall insisted that everyone share a boarding house, where they discussed and wrote the judicial foundations on which the fledgling American democracy was built. Marshall only allowed alcohol when it was raining, though on sunny days, he would famously speculate that it was likely raining somewhere in this vast territory and proceed to pour everyone a glass of Madeira.

The Marshall House is now a museum, kept in remarkably pristine condition from the time the man lived there by Preservation Virginia, the nonprofit that owns the house and provides tours. When checking in at the desk in the basement, glance to your left and behold the cellar that housed the hooch on which the American judiciary was built.

Address 818 East Marshall Street, Richmond, VA 23219, +1 (804) 648-7998, www.preservationvirginia.org/historic-sites/john-marshall-house, johnmarshallhouse@preservationvirginia.org | Getting there Bus 1A, 2A, 2B, 2C, 5 to 9th & Marshall Streets | Hours Thu & Fri 10am–2pm, Sat 10am–5pm, Sun 11am–5pm | Tip The tasting room doesn't serve Madeira, but John Marshall would certainly have approved of the wine produced at Upper Shirley Vineyards in Charles City. Grab a bottle and head to the back lawn for a stellar view of a bend in the James River (600 Shirley Plantation Road, Charles City, www.uppershirley.com).

50 Join or Die Knives

Craftsmen of exquisite cutlery

The knives produced at Join or Die are functional pieces of art. Behold, for example, the 11.25-inch integral chef knife, forged from Damascus steel with black and silver lines rippling into a feather pattern separated from a handle of black Macassar ebony by a ring of pink Rosetta jasper. It is simply beautiful. On the cuter side, tough little shuckers fashioned from local materials, like bourbon barrels, tobacco warehouse beams, and cherry wood from Hollywood Cemetery, can pry open any Chesapeake oyster. Through the permutations of their materials and features, each knife has a personality as intricate as the person who holds it.

The shop could support itself solely by selling its beautiful products, but owner Brent Stubblefield chooses instead to share his craft. "Many knifemakers have a workspace where they can go be alone," he writes on the shop's blog. "We have a community instead. We find our refuge in others as well as in the setting and the work." The name "Join or Die," referencing the severed snake cartoon that American colonists used to promote a united front, a banner of which hangs in the workshop, supports that sentiment.

The dedication to community is also apparent in the classes that Stubblefield and his team host at the shop on certain weekends. Over the course of a day, novices will heat and hammer a six inch block of high-carbon steel into a "blank." Another day is then spent grinding the blank into a shiny blade and joining it to a wooden handle, which is customized to the grip of its maker.

At the end of the weekend, the novice will wipe the sweat from his or her forehead, admire the fruits of their labor, and enjoy a wide range of sensations: the sweet smell of epoxy, the taste of sawdust, the barely audible rip of the blade slicing through a piece of paper, the glint off the bevel, and, most satisfying of all, the feel of a smoothly sanded maple handle against the palm.

Address 1600 Valley Road, Richmond, VA 23222, +1 (804) 852-0392,
www.joinordieknives.com | Getting there Bus 5 to Oliver Hill Way & Hospital Street |
Hours Mon–Fri 9am–5pm | Tip To continue your metalworking journey, find a follow-up
class at the Central Virginia Blacksmith Guild in Goochland (2748 Dogtown Road,
Goochland, www.cvbg.org).

51 Keeble Observatory

View the Cosmos from the Center of the Universe

Stepping from the pitch-black night into the soft, red glow of the Keeble Observatory feels like walking into an '80s sci-fi movie. With the push of a button, an astronomy student sends the contraption into beautifully choreographed motion. The silver dome overhead begins revolving one way, while the telescope in center spins the other. The optical tube tilts up, changing its gaze from Jupiter and its moons to the Orion Nebula.

A line of about 25 people, ranging in life-phase from toddler to senior citizen, perform a sort of conga line around the perimeter of the cylinder, each taking a turn to climb the ladder and take a peek until everyone has seen enough of Orion. With another push of the button, the telescope switches to Mars, and the conga line resumes.

Through this telescope, mere Earthlings can view the Heavens from a special perch in Ashland, Virginia, a township of 7,500 proud inhabitants, who call it the Center of the Universe. The observatory carries forward a centuries-old legacy of interstellar inquiry at Randolph-Macon College, a small liberal arts school, where astronomy has been taught since 1872, not long after the discovery of Neptune. An observatory has been present at the site since 1890, and the original telescope remains on display at the entrance of the new facility.

In 2016, the college rebuilt the observatory, which now houses a Ritchey-Chrétien telescope with a 40-centimeter primary lens, the largest between Washington, DC and the Blue Ridge Mountains. On clear winter nights, the telescope allows the viewing of objects several million light years away, well beyond the reaches of the Milky Way. Although the observatory is primarily used as a laboratory, the public is welcome to weekly stargazing sessions. To plan your visit, check the Keeble Observatory's Instagram feed for weather updates and information about special events.

Address 202 Henry Street, Ashland, VA 23005, +1 (804) 752-3210, www.rmc.edu/departments/physics/keeble-observatory, michaelrodruck@rmc.edu | Getting there By car, take I-95 North to the Ashland/Hanover exit and follow Route 54 west to US Route 1, turn right onto Washington Highway then turn left on Caroline Street and proceed to the destination | Hours Thu 8–9:30pm | Tip In addition to being Ashland's tongue-in-cheek nickname, the Center of the Universe also refers to its best-known brewing company. Visit the brewery, grab a Pocahoptas, and plop down at a picnic table in the beer garden (11293 Air Park Road, Ashland, www.cotubrewing.com).

52 Keystone Truck & Tractor Museum

Horsepower of a different color

If the vehicles of Richard Scarry's children's classic *Cars and Trucks and Things That Go* came to life and drove into a 125,000 square-foot warehouse, the result would closely resemble the Keystone Truck & Tractor Museum in Colonial Heights. There is, alas, no baboon in a banana car or earthworm in an apple, but the 1925 Thermosmobile in the form of that eponymous drinking vessel that "keeps hot hot and cold cold" could've been plucked straight from Mr. Scarry's pages.

The space is roomy and bright with a fresh scent of rubber from the wheels of giant, gleaming machines lined up in every direction. There's no rust, no dirt, no cobwebs; each machine is as glossy and polished as the day they rolled out of the factory 50 to 100 years ago. They're lined up by make, and since each brand had its signature color, you'll find an explosion of color in streaks of bright, bold John Deere greens, McCormick reds, Minneapolis-Moline yellows, and Allis-Chalmers oranges.

The roughly 400 antique cars, tractors, fire trucks, delivery trucks, and tractor trailers here have been lovingly collected and restored by Keith Jones, who fell in love with tractors while hauling lumber for his father's sawmill. When Keith's aunt announced she would auction off his favorite 1950 John Deere Model M tractor, she made him bid just like everyone else, but for $1,400, the future curator secured the prized tractor, the first of hundreds now on display at his museum.

In the international section, look for the stylish, orange and blue '62 Lamborghini and the classic, guards-red '57 Porsche – tractors, of course. Before founding two of the world's most famous sports cars, Ferruccio Lamborghini and Ferdinand Porsche engineered farming equipment, and Keystone has two fine examples of their early work.

Address 880 W Roslyn Road, Colonial Heights, VA 23834, +1 (804) 524-0020, www.keystonetractorworks.com, bonesstone@gmail.com | Getting there By car, take I-95 South to exit 53 toward Southpark Boulevard and then right onto W Roslyn Road; bus PAT Freedom Express to Petersburg Transfer Station and then South Park Mall bus to Roslyn Road & Roslyn Court | Hours Daily 9am–5pm | Tip Nearby, is Pocahontas Island, whose welcome sign claims it is "the oldest Black community in the United States." The Pocahontas Island Black History Museum, which closed with the passing of its owner in 2023, was a stop on the Underground Railroad (224 Witten Street, Petersburg, www.nps.gov/articles/pocaisla.htm).

53 The Kickstand
Gatekeepers of the Capital Trail

From Lewis Ginter's Lakeside Wheel Club of the 1890s to the UCI World Championships in 2015, Richmond has a storied love affair with the bicycle. One of the city's finest municipal accomplishments over the past two decades was the opening of the Capital Trail, a 51.7 mile paved bike path connecting Richmond to Jamestown. With views of the James, passage through verdant forests by the homes of three US presidents, and 44 historical markers describing 400 years of Virginia history, the trail is an excellent way to enjoy the two defining features of the region: its history and its natural beauty.

Near the Richmond end of the Cap Trail, in an otherwise empty lot on the river between Shockoe Bottom and Rocketts Landing, sits a simple, mint-green shipping container called the Kickstand, which rents bikes. For folks without a bike or wanting to demo something a little fancier like a clip-in road bike, an electric bike, or a pull-behind trailer for the kiddos, the Kickstand has a wide variety of affordable rentals in increments of 1, 4, 8, or 24 hours.

The Kickstand is an extension of the Richmond Cycling Corps (RCC), a non-profit dedicated to integrating bicycling into the community, particularly with young people who live in the public housing neighborhoods of East Richmond. The RCC empowers individuals recruited from these communities by hiring them to manage the Kickstand during peak hours.

The RCC runs several other programs, most notably the Legacy Cycling program, an intensive training program through which kids learn to compete in road racing and mountain biking. About ten individuals are enrolled at any given time, riding most days in preparation for races around the state. On a weekend day, you can swing by the Kickstand to enjoy a chat with these young folks, and while you're at it, go ahead and rent a bike to explore the sites along the Cap.

Address 3011 Water Street, Richmond, VA 23223, +1 (804) 372-7813, www.richmondcyclingcorps.org/kickstand, info@richmondcyclingcorps.org | Getting there Bus 4A, 4B, Pulse to Main Street & East Riverfront | Hours Daily 10am–5pm | Tip Near the trailhead of the Richmond Capital Trail is the Great Shiplock Park, a walk along the entry point for boats from the James River into the historic Kanawha Canal. The trail connects to little-known Chapel Island, which features great views of the river (2803 Dock Street, www.jamesriverpark.org/explore-the-park-great-shiplock-park-chapel-island).

54 Klaus Family Tree House

Cultivate big dreams at the Children's Garden

With a little imagination, the walk from the Lotus Bridge to the Cloud Tower of the Klaus Family Tree House can feel like a magical quest. There is so much to see in this one section of the Lewis Ginter Botanical Garden that it's easy to get lost, even for a fully formed adult literate enough to read signs and armed with a map. The area feels designed for a good wander, an immersion into a verdant world where surprises wait around every corner.

For those with a little more time on their hands, several interactive features exist along the way, including the Garden Keeper's Cottage where a master gardener is sometimes on hand to offer secrets to nurturing plants. At the Saunders Farm Garden, you can help grow and harvest fruits and vegetables, which are then provided to Richmonders in need. The Discovery Breezeway, where kids can explore the interaction of animals, weather, and natural materials in cultivating a healthy and productive farm, is built into the garden's original carriage house.

Like hobbits en route to Mordor, travelers along the aptly named Adventure Pathway in search of the Tree House tower will encounter settings of great variety, including the prairie, the butterfly meadow, and the evergreen forest. On a hot day, a detour at the WaterPlay park can help energize a weary wayfarer, as can a rest under the 100-year-old mulberry tree.

Adventurers will eventually reach the universally accessible ramp that winds its way up into the foliage and between towering timbers to the two cylindrical structures rising up like the turrets of a castle. From the deck of the Canopy Room, the voyager can spy the ripples of fish and turtles surfacing in Sydnor Lake. One final climb up the spiral staircase into the Cloud Tower, and the brave wanderer can finally rest, peer through panoramic windows, and survey from a bird's eye view all the stops along their journey.

Address 1800 Lakeside Avenue, Henrico, VA 23228, +1 (804) 262-9887, www.lewisginter.org, contactus@lewisginter.org | **Getting there** By car, take I-95 North to exit 80, turn right onto Hermitage Road to the destination | **Hours** See website for seasonal hours | **Tip** Another phenomenal playground is Park365, an extension of the Soar365, a nonprofit dedicated to empowering Richmonders with disabilities. Park365 also features an accessible treehouse, in addition to a merry-go-round, supportive swing-sets, sensory play areas, and calming gardens and water features (3600 Saunders Avenue, www.soar365.org/park365).

55 Leigh Street Armory

Fortress in the heart of Jackson Ward

With its crenellated roof and circular turrets, the Leigh Street Armory looks like a medieval fortress. Since its construction in 1895, the building has played several roles – armory, school, canteen, museum – all in service to the Black citizens of Richmond. Much like the community it serves, the Armory has survived a multitude of challenges but stands today as an architectural emblem of Richmond's Black history.

The Armory was constructed by the bricklaying company owned by Armstead Walker (1860–1915), husband of bank president, editor, and civil rights leader Maggie L. Walker (1864–1934), to house the First Battalion Virginia Volunteer Armory, a reserve militia composed of Black Richmonders, who used the structure to store weapons and perform training drills. Unsettled by the assembly of armed Black citizens, the Virginia Legislature passed a law disbanding such groups in 1899, and the building ceased its operation as an armory.

In 1899, the Armory was a segregated school for Black students for much of the 20th century. During World War II, the building was again used in a military capacity as a canteen for Black soldiers. Following the war, it resumed operations as a school until integration in the 1950s, at which point it was abandoned and fell into disrepair. In the 1980s, it was purchased by the Black History Museum and Cultural Center of Virginia. Following extensive renovations, the museum became fully operational in 2016.

The museum is thematically split into two. The first floor features the painful journey of Black Richmonders through enslavement, Jim Crow, and modern-day discrimination, and the second floor is dedicated to the triumphs of the community's prominent citizens. As a character itself in the story of Richmond's Black community, the Armory serves as the perfect vessel to explore the important contributions of its neighbors to their city.

Address 122 W Leigh Street, Richmond, VA 23220, +1 (804) 780-9093,
www.blackhistorymuseum.org, info@blackhistorymuseum.org | Getting there Bus 1, 2A,
2B, 2C, 3C to Chamberlain Parkway & Price Street | Hours Wed–Sat 10am–5pm | Tip
After visiting the museum, take your appetite around the block to Mama J's, Richmond's
most heralded soul food restaurant (415 N 1st Street, www.mamajskitchen.com).

56 Madison's Necklace
Fibers from a Founding Father

On your way to the most interesting artifact once belonging to a famous Virginian at the Virginia Museum of History and Culture (VMHC), you'll breeze by Pocahontas' gold buttons, Washington's personal diary, Patrick Henry's eyeglasses, John Marshall's justice robe, the broken death mask of John Tyler, and Arthur Ashe's tennis racquet before you arrive at a necklace belonging to James Madison (1751–1836). What makes this otherwise modest piece of jewelry remarkable, other than having belonged to the fourth president and author of the US Constitution, is the material from which it is weaved: his own hair.

The exact circumstances of the necklace's creation are not known, but its provenance can be traced back through a series of owners to Eleanor Conway "Nelly" Madison Hite (1760–1802), Madison's little sister. The shortest president was typically painted wearing a white powdered wig, but the necklace reveals that he actually sported a mane of abundant, light brown hair. The necklace is a queue string necklace, interwoven with gold studs. Given its intricacy, it was likely weaved together by a professional.

Most history museums have a collection of hair in their holdings. Among the storied strands of many ordinary Virginians, the VMHC also has locks belonging to the Marquis de Lafayette, President Andrew Jackson, and not only Robert E. Lee but also his horse Traveller. In the 18th and 19th centuries, locks of hair served as tokens of affection or, after death, as part of mourning rituals.

This necklace is perhaps the most curious curiosity in a museum filled with an amazing tapestry of Virginia history. The origins of the museum date back to Madison's lifetime, having opened in 1831 as the Virginia Historical Society. In 2022, the VMHC reopened following a massive renovation as one of the country's most impressive history museums.

Address 428 N Arthur Ashe Boulevard, Richmond, VA 23220, +1 (804) 340-1800, www.virginiahistory.org, info@virginiahistory.org | Getting there Bus 20 to Robinson Street & Kensington Avenue | Hours Daily 10am–5pm | Tip A few blocks north of the VMHC, you will find the Devil's Triangle, which got its name in the 1980s for the rough and rowdy bars, where scoundrels convened after hours. In the last couple of decades, a new group of bars and restaurants have rehabbed the rep of the diminutive neighborhood (corner of N Sheppard Street at Park Avenue, www.devilstrianglerva.com).

57 Maggie Walker House

Home of Richmond's favorite daughter

No one personifies the struggles and triumphs of Black Richmonders through the Reconstruction and Jim Crow eras like Maggie Walker (1864–1934). In a story befitting a Hollywood period piece, Walker was born at the peak of the Civil War inside the Church Hill mansion of famed Union spy Elizabeth van Lew (1818–1900), from the nebulous and short-lived union of her mother, an enslaved Black woman who did Ms. Van Lew's laundry, and a white Confederate soldier.

After a short career as a teacher, Walker joined and rose through the ranks of the Independent Order of St. Luke's, a national fraternal organization focused on the economic and social empowerment of the Black community. She became its leader in 1899 and took the organization from the brink of bankruptcy to nationwide success, while also raising her family in a townhouse in Jackson Ward.

With Black citizens facing structural barriers to banking and commerce, Walker mobilized her community to open its own institutions, ultimately transforming Jackson Ward into the prosperous epicenter of Richmond's Black society. There, she personally opened a department store, a newspaper, and a bank, the first one chartered by a Black woman in the US. For the cultural and economic prominence that Walker helped cultivate in Jackson Ward, the neighborhood became known as the Harlem of the South and Black Wall Street.

Evidence of Walker's legacy is abundant in Richmond, but for a glimpse into her professional and family life, visit her former home at the intersection of "Quality Row" and "The Deuce" aka Leigh Street and 2nd Street. Proud of her accomplishments after coming up "on the rough side of the mountain," as she would state, Walker kept her first floor well-appointed to project success for prominent visitors like WEB Dubois and Booker T. Washington. The home is kept nearly exactly as it was in the mid-1930s, when Walker died here.

Address 600 N 2nd Street, Richmond, VA 23219, +1 (804) 771-2017,
www.nps.gov/mawa/index.htm | Getting there Bus 1, 2A, 2B, 2C to 1st & Leigh Streets |
Hours Tue–Sat 9am–4:30pm | Tip Following Mrs. Walker's lead of bringing together
the Jackson Ward community, nearby Urban Hang Suite is a social café with a busy front
room where customers can commune while getting their caffeine fix (304 E Broad Street,
www.urbanhangsuiterva.com).

58   Manchester Climbing Wall
Ruins with a modern purpose

The old Richmond & Petersburg Railroad used to head south out of the city over the James River on a train trestle built in 1838. During the Fall of Richmond on April 2, 1865, the Confederate army burned the bridge down, but the tall granite abutment on the south side and the stone piers across the river withstood the blazes. The bridge was rebuilt after the war and remained functional until the 1970s, when it was torn down. The same structures that had survived the war remained, and in the 1980s, Richmonders repurposed the ruins as a rock climbing park.

From a climbing perspective, the diversity and technicality of the area are well-regarded for a park set in the middle of a city. The aforementioned 60-foot wall is the main attraction, hosting 20 different routes that range in skill level on the Yosemite Decimal System from the 5.4-rated (easy) Gutterball, so-called because the climber is gently nestled into a 90-degree corner providing two faces worth of handholds, to the 5.10d (hard) aptly-named Tendonitis. Three of the routes contain anchors at the top and are thus suitable for toprope climbing.

The piers dotted across the river provide yet more climbing terrain. The three closest to the south bank have bolts set into their walls, allowing for sport climbing routes. For climbers seeking solitude and in possession of a seafaring vessel, there are another three piers with named trad climbing routes out in the middle of the river.

The remnants of the 19th century are literally everywhere in Richmond, but it is special to see these weathered structures repurposed into something so modern and practical. You can park close to the wall, but there are two more picturesque ways to get there: the southern route via the Manchester Floodwall or the northern route across the T. Tyler Potterfield Bridge. Either will provide stunning views of the city and the river.

Address Southern end of the T. Tyler Potterfield Memorial Bridge, Richmond, VA 23224, +1 (804) 646-8911, www.jamesriverpark.org/explore-the-park-manchester-climbing-wall, friends@jamesriverpark.org | **Getting there** Bus 2A, 2B, 2C to Semmes Avenue & 10th Street | **Hours** Unrestricted | **Tip** For toprope climbing in a more modern setting, check out Peak Experiences, a state-of-the-art gym featuring 50-foot-tall walls. The club has several programs for kids as young as eight (1375 Overbrook Road, www.peakexperiences.com).

59 Manchester Docks

Where enslaved Africans first met the New World

Behind the large, granite seawall that comprises the Manchester Docks is a well-worn, dirt path shaded by oaks and paralleling the curve of the gently flowing James. The peaceful setting contrasts sharply with the horrors that occurred here centuries ago, when tens of thousands of men, women, and children were forced to walk the path against their will.

Sometime in the 1600s, ships from Guinea, The Gambia, and Sierra Leone began arriving at the Manchester Docks with kidnapped Africans, and the estimated 80% who survived the "Middle Passage" first set foot onto American soil at this location. From there, groups of up to 200 human beings, shackled at the neck and chained together, were marched in lines across the Mayo Bridge and through downtown to the jails at 15th and Franklin Streets. This procession occurred under the cover of darkness so that polite Richmond society would not have to bear the sight and smell of these people, malnourished, bearing open wounds, and covered in the filth that had accumulated under overcrowded decks.

In 1807, the federal Act Prohibiting Importation of Slaves rendered the plantations of Virginia the most abundant source of enslaved people to the rest of the Southern states, and from 1830-1860, Richmond was the nation's largest marketplace. Enslavers from across Virginia auctioned up to 50 people per day at the markets downtown, wherefrom they completed the march of their ancestors in reverse, eventually boarding ships moored at the Manchester Docks bound for plantations in states far away from their families, whom they would likely never see again.

These days, the Manchester Docks are the starting point of the Richmond Slave Trail. On this path, Richmonders can retrace the steps of their ancestors and collectively acknowledge the city's shameful leadership in this terrible chapter in American history.

Address 1200 Branders Street, Richmond, VA 23224, www.jamesriverpark.org/explore-the-park-ancarrows-landing-historic-manchester-slave-docks | Getting there By car, take I-95 to exit 73 and turn right onto Maury Street to the destination | Hours Daily dawn–dusk | Tip Lumpkin's Jail, the downtown Richmond compound where many of the enslaved persons were held, was also called the Devil's Half-Acre because of the brutal methods of its owner Robert Lumpkin. Mary Lumpkin, whom Lumpkin once enslaved, inherited the site and laid the groundwork for Virginia Union University, an HBCU (1509-1547 E Broad Street, www.visitrichmondva.com/listing/lumpkins-jail/11210).

60 Meadowgate Alpacas
The cutest herd this side of the Andes

"It's just really easy to fall in love with alpacas," says Nicole Phillips, who, along with her husband Stephen, owns Meadowgate Alpacas in Beaverdam, Virginia, about 30 minutes north of Richmond. Sign up for an hour-long farm visit, offered to private groups of up to 10 people from April through December, and you will assuredly fall in love too.

The butterflies will begin to flutter from the moment you pat the dense fleece on the neck of Phoenix, the handsome herdsire, to the moment you lock eyes with Zendaya, with her head propped on the fence to catch a peek at you. By the time baby Twilight, a new addition to the herd in 2023, nuzzles into your neck, Cupid's arrow will be lodged firmly in your backside.

The Philipses began their love affair with alpacas in 2017. Once owners of a horse farm north of Boston, they moved to Virginia in 2005 and sold their last horses in 2015. After taking a break from raising farm animals, they happened upon an alpaca farm. It was the first time Stephen had ever spent time with an alpaca, but he fell hard. That same day, the couple decided to purchase their first three alpacas, the progenitors of a herd that has since grown to 30.

The Philipses happily share their love of alpacas with the community in a variety of ways. In addition to hosting visitors to the farm, they also provide outreach to local organizations in the form of "alpaca therapy," bringing alpacas on visits to senior living facilities, veterans' groups, and nonprofits focused on children with special needs. With the fleece collected from the annual shearing, usually in April, Meadowgate also produces garments, yarn, and home goods available for purchase online. Many of these products are sourced back to one specific alpaca, so when you fall in love during a farm visit, it's possible to own a special memento from your fleecy crush.

Address 16305 Coatesville Road, Beaverdam, VA 23015, +1 (804) 432-3572, www.meadowgatealpacas.com, nicole@meadowgatealpacas.com | Getting there By car, take I-295 North to US-33 West to VA-671 towards Beaverdam | Hours See website for visit schedule | Tip Just over a mile east from Meadowgate is Patrick Henry's Scotchtown, the house where the "orator of the American Revolution" lived from 1771 to 1778 and where he likely wrote the famous words that launched the war for independence (16120 Chiswell Lane, Beaverdam, www.preservationvirginia.org/historic-sites/patrick-henrys-scotchtown).

61 Mekong
Unlikely birthplace of Richmond's craft brew scene

Mekong's spring rolls and claypot chicken are undoubtedly delicious, but the food is not the feature that has earned its many plaudits. That would be its draft beer selection and the incredible story of how a Vietnamese restaurant in a strip mall on an objectively unsexy stretch of West Broad Street sparked the revival of the city's dormant brewing industry.

Over the centuries, Richmond breweries have had a long and tragic history, ebbing and flowing with the events of the nation. The city's first known brewery was burned to the ground by Benedict Arnold's forces in 1781. In the rebirth of the city after the Civil War, David Yuengling, Jr. left his father's famous brewery in Philly to open his own in Richmond, the James River Steam Cellars, which folded during the Panic of 1873. Prohibition put the brakes on another boom in the 20th century, and by 2006, only one craft brewery, Legend, remained in operation.

That was the same year that An Bui, owner of Mekong, began serving eclectic draft beers from around the world. In a beer-drinking city without a brewing scene, his 55 taps amassed a community of enthusiasts from Richmond and beyond. Two of those patrons were Eric McKay and Patrick Murtaugh, out-of-towners who, after meeting up at Mekong and witnessing the city's beer fandom, chose Richmond as the site of their Hardywood Brewery, which opened in 2011.

The following year, the duo lobbied for legislation allowing brew houses to serve their product onsite, paving the way for the explosion of more than 40 local breweries that have since opened. That was also the year that the craftbeer.com inaugural "Great American Beer Bar" award went to Mekong, as it did for the next two years. In 2014, Bui opened up his own brewery adjacent to the restaurant called the Answer, a reference to Mekong's long standing motto, "Beer is the Answer!"

Address 6004 W Broad Street, Richmond, VA 23230, +1 (804) 288-8929, www.mekongisforbeerlovers.com, anmekong@aol.com | Getting there Bus 19 to Broad Street & Crestwood Avenue | Hours Sun–Thu 11am–9pm, Fri & Sat 11am–10pm | Tip The ruins of Yuengling's failed James River Steam Brewery are still present in Rockett's Landing. All that remains of the towering 80-foot factory is an elaborate cellar and its arched opening onto Old Main Street, though this is currently fenced off (5 Steam Brewery Court).

62 The Mighty Wurlitzer

The voice of Richmond's movie palace

Everything at the Byrd Theatre glows and glistens, from the 18-foot, Czechoslovakian crystal chandelier, to the gilded Lyon & Healy harp sitting in an alcove, to the Greek deities depicted in murals along its walls. This stunning visual experience deserves an audio counterpart equally splendid, which is supplied by a magnificent pipe organ known as the Mighty Wurlitzer. When its platform ascends from the orchestra pit, the Wurlitzer beams proudly centerstage, like a powerful opera singer belting to an adoring audience.

The Byrd opened its doors on Christmas Eve 1928 and the Wurlitzer made its big debut that same evening. Originally installed to provide the audio for the silent films of the era, the Wurlitzer functions as a "one-person orchestra," whose musical dexterity can provide a versatile soundtrack. An incredible feat of engineering, the Wurlitzer consists of a console joined by hidden magnetic and pneumatic connections to an entire orchestra, including: 17 ranks of organ pipes rising four stories on both sides of the stage, a tuba, trumpet, xylophone, mandolin, drums, tambourines, sleigh bells, a bird whistle, a train whistle, an automobile horn, and horses' hooves, among many others. The organist and console appear detached from the orchestra housed in rooms above the stage, invisible to the crowd.

One person controls this entire apparatus, and since 1996 that person has been Bob Gulledge, 13th in the lineage of Wurlitzer maestros at the Byrd. These days, he warms up the crowd of up to 1,300 sitting in springy, red-velvet seats. Gulledge speaks of the Wurlitzer with a love one typically has for an elderly family member, and he deeply appreciates its role in the theater. As he said in a video tour in 2020, "There are … a lot of things about the Byrd that give it its character and its personality, but it's the organ that gives the theater a voice."

Address 2908 W Cary Street, Richmond, VA 23221, +1 (804) 358-3056, www.byrdtheatre.org | Getting there Bus 5, 20, 78 to Cary & Sheppard Streets | Hours See website for showtimes | Tip Before the show, grab *un croque monsieur et moules frites* at Can Can Brasserie, just two blocks west from the Byrd. It pairs especially well with the Byrd's French Film Festival held annually in March (3120 W Cary Street, www.cancanrva.com).

63 Monumental Church
Memorial to Richmond's worst disaster

On the night after Christmas, 1811, a crowd of more than 600 packed into the Richmond Theater to watch the season's last performance of the Placide and Green Theater Company. After the first act of a pantomime called *The Bleeding Nun*, as a chandelier was hoisted, its cords became entangled within its arms, pulling lit candles against a piece of scenery. Within minutes, the entire building was engulfed in flames.

The structure had specifically been rebuilt to be fireproof, but its layout proved to be catastrophic, particularly for the more affluent patrons trapped on the balcony. By the time the flames were subdued, at least 72 individuals had perished, marking the deadliest urban disaster up till that point in the life of the young nation. Due to the high number of casualties and difficulty identifying them, the dead were all interred together in a large, brick crypt. The city commissioned Robert Mills (1781–1855), architect of the Washington Monument, to build a memorial over the crypt in the form of Monumental Church.

The church is no longer in use, but the nonprofit organization Preservation Virginia has taken ownership and welcomes visitors. Tours start on the front porch, which holds an ornamental structure engraved with the names of the victims, arranged curiously by gender and social class. The porch opens into the enormous, octagonal vestibule of the church under a wide saucer dome, which provides for some baffling acoustics in the space. Walking toward the chancel, visitors will pass by the pews of two well-known parishioners, John Marshall and Edgar Allan Poe, and into a small doorway to the left of the sanctuary. A narrow hallway wraps around to a staircase that descends into a chilly, unfinished basement. At the bottom of the staircase, there lies the crypt, a large, brick rectangle standing just as it did in 1812, its inhabitants undisturbed.

Address 1224 E Broad Street, Richmond, VA 23219, +1 (804) 643-7407, www.historicrichmond.com/property/monumental-church | Getting there Bus Pulse to VCU Medical Center Eastbound Station or bus 1A, 1B, 1C, 7A, 7B, 29X, 56, 64X to Broad & 11th Streets | Hours By appointment only | Tip Across Broad Street sits the former Charlotte Williams Memorial Hospital, which contains an empty and very eerie surgical amphitheater from 1899. The building is now used by VDOT, and tours of the amphitheater are conducted with their permission (1201 E Broad Street, www.dhr.virginia.gov/historic-registers/127-0395).

64 Mount Malady
First English hospital in the New World

In the third year of Jamestown's existence, things were going very badly there. Conditions during the winter of 1609-1610, also known as the "Starving Time," became so bleak that colonists resorted to eating horses, dogs, rats, and even the remains of other colonists. Seeking greener pastures, the Virginia Company sent Sir Thomas Dale (1570–1619) from England with 300 men in tow to settle a new seat for the colony, a village 60 miles upriver that he named the "Citie of Henricus."

The village ultimately lasted from 1611-1622, when it was abandoned after the devastating Indian Massacre of 1622, but long enough for the colonists to expand further west and create a permanent foothold on the continent. In 1613, at a site called Coxsondale a few miles south of Henricus, the settlers built Mount Malady, the first English hospital in the New World. The 40-bed building served primarily as a barracks and receiving facility for the new colonists needing rest and recuperation after the rough journey across the Atlantic. But it earned its name for also treating the early colonial ailments, including typhoid, dysentery, and malaria.

The exact location of Mount Malady is not known, but you can access the next closest thing. In 1985, a group of historians built a recreation of the village, now known as the Henricus Historical Park. Their rendition of the hospital is a long building, austere and dimly lit, with several patient beds leading to an enormous fireplace at the far end. Adjacent to the building is the Physick Garden, where yarrow, betony, tansy, lemon balm, wormwood, lavender, and sage are grown for their medicinal properties, as they may have been in 1613. Surgical instruments, looking very much like medieval implements of torture, are laid out on a table. A visit to Mount Malady will remind modern guests that life in the present day is not actually that bad.

Address 251 Henricus Park Road, Chester, VA 23836, +1 (804) 748-1611,
www.henricus.org | Getting there By car, take I–95 South to exit 61A onto SR-10 East then
turn left onto Old Stage Road, right onto Coxendale Road, and right onto Henricus Park
Road | Hours Wed–Sun 10am–5pm | Tip Not far from Henricus, and halfway between
Richmond and Petersburg, is the Half Way House, a tavern serving weary travelers since
before the Revolutionary War to the present day (10301 Jefferson Davis Highway, North
Chesterfield, www.halfwayhouserestaurant.com).

65 The Necessary House

When ya gotta go, why go it alone?

Westover Plantation in Charles City was the seat (pun not intended, but appreciated) of the prominent Byrd family starting in the 1680s. Around 1750, William Byrd II, the founder of the City of Richmond, built Westover's stunning Georgian mansion overlooking the James River, and along with it, a very unique outhouse. "The Necessary House" is a small, brick building with one approximately eight-by-eight-foot room. Inside, you'll find a fireplace flanked by two wooden toilets facing a semicircular bench with three more. You counted correctly. In this tiny room, there are five places to do one's business, all within a few feet of each other and separated by absolutely nothing. It would have been well-lit by the luminescence of a cozy fire.

Although a man of great accomplishment, Byrd's own diaries depict his darker nature, including cruel treatment of the enslaved people at Westover. You may consider whether the unusual design of the outhouse is related to the man's odd nature and just who the Necessary House was intended to serve. Historians do not believe the Byrd family would have inconvenienced themselves or their prominent guests with an outdoor bathroom and would have instead used toilet chairs inside the house. Furthermore, the servants would likely have had their own pit latrines adjacent to their quarters. Who, then, was sitting fireside in the party potty?

One theory suggests that, since the Byrd patriarchs were commanders of the local militia that frequently visited Westover and stayed camped out in the backyard, the privy was built for the soldiers, who must have been thankful never to wait in line to hit the head after a hard day's work. Adding to the intrigue, there is a structurally identical building across the yard that has fallen into disrepair, suggesting there may have been a second Necessary House for the wives of the militiamen.

Address 7000 Westover Road, Charles City, VA 23030, +1 (804) 829-2882, www.historicwestover.com, info@historicwestover.com | Getting there By car, take I-64 East to exit 200 onto I-295 South then take exit 22A onto SR-5 East, right onto Herring Creek Road, and left onto Westover Road | Hours Daily 10am–4:30pm | Tip Even older than the mansion at Westover is the nearby church house that shares its name. Union troops reportedly used the headstones there for the floors of their military tents, while their horses stayed inside the church (6401 John Tyler Memorial Highway, Charles City, www.westoverepiscopalchurch.org).

66 New Pump-House
Haunted castle on the James

On March 6, 2010, paranormalist Robert Bess showed up to the first floor of the James River Park's New Pump-House with his ghost-capturing machine, the Parabot. It's a seven-foot, plexiglass rectangle resembling a phone booth, complete with a Tesla coil emanating green light and conjuring memories of Slimer from *Ghostbusters*. There, before 145 curious attendees, Bess proved the building was haunted. To be clear, the Parabot failed to detect any ghosts but only because, according to Bess, *too much* paranormal activity overwhelmed the machine. The Pump-House, he contended, is not just a run-of-the-mill haunted locale but, indeed, an entire portal to the spirit world.

Regardless of the Parabot's conclusions, the magnificent, Gothic-revival structure, nicknamed the Castle on the James, certainly looks like it could be haunted. The Pump-House was built in 1883 to pump 13 million gallons of drinking water each day from the James River and Kanawha Canal into the Byrd Park Reservoir. In the decades that ensued, it also became a community gathering spot. Gilded Age Richmonders would take flat-bottom boats from downtown up the canal to attend parties in the open-air ballroom on the second floor. When its technology became obsolete, the building was shuttered in 1924, gradually falling into disrepair and apparently opening its doors to otherworldly visitors.

These days, volunteers with Friends of the Pump-House are busy restoring the facility and recently received a $1,000,000 federal grant for its renovation. The group leads monthly hard-hat tours through the building and sponsors special events, like Poe at the Pump-House. There are high hopes that the building can be restored to its former glory. In the meantime, you can walk the trail that runs west from the Pump-House along the canal or peak through the windows for a glimpse at inhabitants from another realm.

Address 1708 Pump House Drive, Richmond, VA 23221, +1 (804) 646-5733, www.friendsofpumphouse.org | Getting there Bus 78 to Meadow Street & Nevada Avenue | Hours Daily 8am–7pm | Tip A trip aboard a flat-bottom boat is still available to those wishing to travel the Kanawha Canal downtown. Riverfront Canal Cruises offers 40-minute guided tours about the rich history along the canal (139 Virginia Street, www.venturerichmond.com/our-services/riverfront-canal-cruises).

67 Outpost Richmond

Bike shop and bodega for the everyday rider

Putting a bike shop and a grocery store under one roof may seem like an unusual business model, but Outpost owner Braden Govoni has found a subtle symbiosis between the two: bike customers getting a tune-up need basic provisions, and frequent grocery shoppers may someday want to buy a bike. Govoni started Outpost to provide a more laidback bike shop experience to a city saturated with "racing bike culture" and discovered that everyday cyclists appreciated a few fridges full of food and beer.

A blog post circa the launch of Outpost in 2015 explains, "Bike shops often come off as exclusive, snobby, or a boys club … so this is a fresh start. I want to be the shop that riders of all ages and abilities feel comfortable walking into." Govoni worked in other bike shops prior to starting Outpost and split off to cater to a more lowkey clientele. As he told Richmond cyclist Trey Dunnaville on the *Wheel Community* podcast in 2023, "I don't wanna sell bikes, I wanna sell biking …. I wanna be a gateway to riding. I don't wanna scare people off by being this high-end thing. I don't want to have high-end bikes … [and] lots of fancy cycling kits on the wall because that's intimidating."

Complementing the racks of relatively affordable bikes, the grocery side of the shop feels like a big-city bodega with a very Richmond spin. The shelves are stocked with everyday foodstuffs and libations, mostly from right here in the RVA. Situated at the southwest corner of Forest Hill, Outpost is to that neighborhood what a corner store in NYC is to its city block – a purveyor of staples for neighbors who need a last-minute ingredient or a sixer. Unlike a metropolitan city block, though, Forest Hill is bordered on one side by the Buttermilk Trail and on another by Forest Hill Park, both portals to epic urban biking trails. Bc it bread, booze, or bikes, Outpost has the bases covered.

Address 4813 Forest Hill Avenue, Richmond, VA 23225, +1 (804) 447-1730, www.outpostrichmond.com, info@outpostrichmond.com | Getting there Bus 2A, 2B to Forest Hill Avenue & Westover Hills Boulevard | Hours Mon–Fri 11am–7pm, Sat 10am–7pm, Sun noon–6pm | Tip Forest Hill Park hosts a 10-foot-tall pyramid with mysterious origins. Theories abound – ancient sundial, garden ornament, Confederate memorial, monument to a pet bear, gravestone for enslaved servants? No one quite knows why it's there (4021 Forest Hill Avenue, www.rva.gov/parks-recreation/forest-hill-park).

68 Patrick Henry's Pew

Focal point of American independence

On March 23rd, 1775, the members of the Virginia House of Burgesses who turned up for the Second Virginia Convention at St. John's Church found themselves at a crossroads. Having been subjected to years of economic oppression by a government 3,000 miles away, the colonists debated how best to respond to increasing British belligerence. Patrick Henry, a 38-year-old lawyer and already a well-respected orator, took the floor to advocate for the creation of a militia, a move that would all but declare revolution. The events that followed are described thusly by a clergyman sitting in the pews that day, as recounted in Henry Randall's *The Life of Thomas Jefferson*:

"Henry arose with an unearthly fire burning in his eye. He commenced somewhat calmly—but the smothered excitement began more and more to play upon his features and thrill in the tones of his voice. The tendons of his neck stood out white and rigid like whipcords. His voice rose louder and louder, until the walls of the building and all within them seemed to shake and rock in its tremendous vibrations... His last exclamation—'Give me liberty or give me death'—was like the shout of the leader which turns back the rout of battle!"

These seven words echoed, first into the ears of Washington, Jefferson, and five other signers of the Declaration of Independence present that day. They echoed across the Atlantic to the throne of George III and to the minutemen who took up arms at Lexington and Concord a few weeks later. They continue to echo today in the print of textbooks and the spray paint on walls wherever oppressed people speak out against tyranny.

St. John's, still an active Episcopal Church, hosts daily tours during which you can hear your own voice echo off the same sounding board that hung in the parish in 1775. There are also weekly reenactments of the convention on Sundays during the summer months.

Address 2401 E Broad Street, Richmond, VA 23223, +1 (804) 648-5015,
www.historicstjohnschurch.org | Getting there Bus 4A, 4B, 12 to 25th & Broad Streets |
Hours Thu 11:30am–4pm, Fri & Sat 9:30am–4pm, Sun noon–4pm, Mon 9:30am–4pm |
Tip To settle your stirred passions after the reenactment, head across the street to Patrick
Henry's Pub & Grille, a dimly lit, English-style pub with antebellum Richmond vibes
(2300 E Broad Street, www.thephpub.com).

69_Penny Lane Pub
You'll never walk alone in downtown Richmond

When football is on the telly, Penny Lane comes to life. Although the sign out front reads "Liverpool's Penny Lane Pub," the large, labyrinthine bar has room for football foes of all stripes, as beloved bartender "Chelsea Joe" can attest. Indeed, the pub is the official gathering spot, sanctioned by the clubs themselves, for the Richmond fanbases of Liverpool, Chelsea, and Tottenham Hotspur.

Chelsea fans were the first to secure the designation, but sensing the universe was out of alignment, the Liverpool faithful quickly followed suit. Just don't be caught wearing a Manchester United kit in the northwest corner during a Northwest Derby, lest ye receive an earful of Scouse-tinged scorn from hooligans armed with pints of Smithwicks.

True Liverpudlians here are few and far between but include the pub's founder Terry O'Neill. He played football in Liverpool (though not for *the* Liverpool) and bounced at The Cavern, the club where the famous foursome adorning the walls of Penny Lane got their start. Terry's wife was present at Woolton's Parish Church when John met Paul. While in service of the British Merchant Navy, Terry found his way to New York, and at the urging of other British expats, eventually to Richmond. "When he arrived here, he asked, 'Where are the pubs? Where do the lawyers get together with the carpenters?'" says Terry's son Terence, who now runs the establishment. "This was all built from one man's vision."

O'Neill, a carpenter by trade, quite literally handbuilt the rich wooden inlay that gives the bar its distinctly British feel. Also contributing to the vibe are the low ceilings hung with steins, steaming heaps of shepherd's pie, and walls saturated with equal parts Beatles paraphernalia, Liverpool FC merchandise, and photos of besotted patrons from days of yore. Short of traveling across the pond, there's simply nowhere better for a pint and a match.

Address 421 East Franklin Street, Richmond, VA 23219, +1 (804) 780-1682, www.pennylanepub.com, pennylanepubRVA@gmail.com | Getting there Bus 5, 14 to Main & 5th Streets | Hours Tue & Wed 4pm–midnight, Thu 4pm–2am, Fri 3pm–2am, Sat 11–2am, Sun 11am–9pm | Tip Speaking of places that remind us of Great Britain, "the view that named Richmond" is the vantage in Libby Hill Park, from which city founder William Byrd II reminisced about his English home, Richmond upon Thames (2801 East Franklin Street, www.scenicvirginia.org/view-that-named-richmond).

70 __ Pipeline
Tightrope over the James

Most Richmonders would agree that the James River, the source of our water, centerpiece of our natural splendor, and linchpin of our shared history, is the quintessential feature of the city. Among the best ways to enjoy the James is a stroll along the Pipeline Walkway, a tucked-away, elevated footpath atop a large municipal waste pipe and beneath a train trestle in the heart of downtown Richmond.

The scenery from the Pipeline vantage is remarkable. Along the entirety of the path, you can watch rafters, canoeists, and kayakers navigate the Class IV Pipeline rapids. A little further up is a sandy beach, where people lay out and swim in the warmer months. From large rocks outlining the rapids, anglers cast lines for catfish and striped bass. At the end of the pipe, you can take in the giant arches of the Manchester Bridge spanning the river.

Near the beginning and just across the river is Vauxhall Island, home to one of the few urban great blue heron rookeries, where the lanky iconic birds nest and breed. The island hosts approximately 40 nests, each tended by two herons, made of sticks stacked on one another. The great blues are ever-present in the adjacent Pipeline Rapids, where they stand statue-still until the time comes to spear a fish swimming upstream.

Although the view across the river provides an unmatched serenity, the path itself can be daunting at times. When the river is high, the roar of the whitewater rushing underneath feels overpowering, as does the thunder of a CSX train rumbling overhead. The view of the water moving underfoot, the vastness of the pillars supporting the train trestle, and the narrowness of the walkway can induce a sense of vertigo. It must be noted, though, that the walkway itself, which is only accessible by climbing down a metal ladder, is not suitable for small children, pets, or people with certain physical challenges.

Address 310 S 14th Street, Richmond, VA 23219, www.jamesriverpark.org/explore-the-park-pipeline | Getting there Bus 1A, 1B, 1C to 14th & Dock Streets | Hours Daily dawn–dusk | Tip For another spectacular stroll along the James, head across the river to the Manchester Floodwall Walk. Vistas from atop the floodwall include the city skyline and the underbelly of the Manchester Bridge (south end of the 14th Street Bridge, www.jamesriverpark.org/explore-the-park-floodwall-park).

71 Poe's Childhood Bed

What visions haunted the Raven while lying here?

The Poe Museum is situated in Shockoe Bottom's Old Stone House, the oldest residential building in Richmond, and it contains the world's largest collection of Poe-related materials. The Raven himself visited the house as a child while escorting the Marquis de Lafayette on a parade through the city in 1828. In reality, Poe (1809–1849) was thought to be gregarious and charming, but the vibe in the museum reflects the melancholic, brooding character that predominates his legacy. The doors are creaky, the lighting is dim, the air is cool and still. Two black cats, Edgar and Pluto, seem to appear and vanish out of thin air. A sense of dread permeates the premises.

In a series of three rooms, dedicated chronologically to his childhood, writing career, and death, the Poe museum recreates the 19th century with a vast array of the author's artifacts, including: a pair of his silk socks; the timepiece that ticked in his pocket when he wrote *The Tell-Tale Heart*; the engagement ring engraved with "Edgar" that he gave to Elmira Royster; the trunk holding all his earthly possessions confiscated by a Richmond bar where he owed money in the days before his death; a lock of his hair that was posthumously found to contain arsenic and mercury; and most eerily, the bed where he slept as a boy.

When gazing upon his childhood bed, one cannot help but recall the room depicted in *The Tell-Tale Heart*, in which the narrator watches an elderly man sleep for hours until eventually suffocating him to death. A childhood friend of the writer said that one of Poe's greatest fears was being watched while he slept. You can only wonder what nightmares haunted him as he lay here in the darkness.

If you'd like to commemorate Poe's legacy with friends, music, and libations supplied by a local brewery, the Museum hosts an "Unhappy Hour" on the last Friday evening of every month.

Address 1914 East Main Street, Richmond, VA 23223, +1 (804) 648-5523, www.poemuseum.org, info@poemuseum.org | Getting there Bus 14 to Main & 18th Streets | Hours Tue–Sat 10am–5pm, Sun 11am–5pm | Tip Just a few blocks east of the museum, you'll find one of the best breakfasts in Richmond at Millie's Diner. Enjoy the Devil's Mess (which could've been the name of a Poe short story), a heap of eggs, sausage, cheese, avocado, curry, and Sriracha (2603 East Main Street, www.milliesdiner.com).

72 Pole Green Produce

Preferred purveyor of Hanover's favorite fruit

If Richmond has a signature dish, it may simply be two pieces of bread coated generously with Duke's mayonnaise, sprinkled with salt and pepper, and jammed full of sliced Hanover tomatoes. There's nothing genetically distinct about the Hanover tomato; what counts is where it was grown. Just as true champagne is made exclusively in the region of Champagne, the Hanover tomato is grown exclusively in Hanover County and, more precisely, in the sandy, loamy soil east of I-95.

The region certainly capitalizes on the lore of its favorite fruit. Richmond's upscale eateries work them into their summertime menus, the football teams of bitter rivals Mechanicsville and Patrick Henry high schools square off annually in the "Tomato Bowl," and locals pay homage to their precious produce each July at the Hanover Tomato Festival. Within Hanover, the best place to buy the legendary tomatoes is Pole Green Produce, a large outdoor market that has been owned and operated by the same family since 1986.

Owner Gwen Christian explains the appeal of the Hanover tomato thusly: "The acidity of the soil makes the Hanover Tomato the Hanover Tomato. That acid transfers to the tomato and creates a unique flavor. A little sweet, a lot of acid. It makes an unforgettable tomato. Before you even slice it up to taste the difference, you can smell the difference. You see a lot of people coming in and putting a Hanover right up to their nose to check if they're real and if it's going to taste like how they remember."

Pole Green sources as much of its produce locally as possible, including several summertime crops that Christian raises from seed. The place always seems busy, especially in the warmer months, with loyal locals and statewide visitors alike. As Christian says, "[p]eople know where to go to get quality produce, and they're willing to travel a bit to come to Pole Green to get it."

Address 6547 Pole Green Road, Mechanicsville, VA 23116, +1 (804) 730-7732, www.facebook.com/polegreenproduce | Getting there By car, take the Mechanicsville Turnpike to I-295 North to Pole Green Road | Hours Daily 8am – 6:30pm | Tip Closer to Richmond, the best place to find fresh produce is in Randolph at the Birdhouse Farmers' Market, which bills itself as "the hub of an ecosystem of healthy, food-related community activities." The market is open on Tuesday afternoons May through November (1507 Grayland Avenue, www.birdhousefarmersmarket.org).

73 — Powhatan Stone

A memorial to native Virginia royalty

At the southern edge of Chimborazo Park, from a vantage high atop Church Hill, sits a pedestal propping up a modest slab of stone. According to legend, this nondescript nugget of granite once belonged to the headstone of King Wahunsenacawh, the giant of Virginia history known more familiarly as Chief Powhatan (c. 1547–1618).

From the late 1500s until his death, a period that included the arrival of John Smith (1850–1631) and the settlement of Jamestown, Powhatan ruled a confederation of over 30 Indian tribes in Central and Eastern Virginia. During these tumultuous years, he managed to keep relative peace between native people and the new European arrivals, through, among other means, blessing the marriage of his daughter Pocahontas (c. 1595–1617) to John Rolfe (c. 1585–1622).

Powhatan was reportedly buried beneath an enormous stone overlooking the James River a few miles south of Richmond. In 1911, the descendants of the white settlers who had claimed the land in the 1700s sold their property and donated a portion of the stone to the city. The slab was then set in its current location. An 1881 guidebook to Richmond describes Powhatan's headstone as "a boulder which marks the burial-place of the celebrated Indian potentate, and bears many curious carvings and symbols." Two images of the burial site also exist: a 1903 photograph of the giant boulder and a 1910 postcard depicting its location within a wooden lattice beneath a grouping of trees.

Based on these earlier depictions, the memorial today is less a "boulder" and more a suitcase-sized chunklet, a mere vestige of the headstone once befitting a great king. The stone is also now without out "curious carvings and symbols," as the only man-made marking is the gaudy bronze plaque set into its surface in the 20th century. Despite these discrepancies, the stone perpetuates the memory of a legendary leader.

POWHATAN STONE

AN OLD INDIAN STONE REMOVED FROM AND
NOW OVERLOOKING "POWHATAN SEAT" A ROYAL
RESIDENCE OF KING POWHATAN WHEN CAPTAIN
JOHN SMITH AND HIS FELLOW "ADVENTURERS"
MADE THE FIRST PERMANENT ENGLISH SETTLEMENT
IN THIS COUNTRY AT JAMESTOWN, VIRGINIA 1607.

"POWHATAN SEAT" WAS THE RESIDENCE FROM
1788-1865 OF THE ANCESTORS OF PETER H. MAYO
BY WHOSE DAUGHTERS THIS STONE WAS
PRESENTED TO THE ASSOCIATION FOR THE
PRESERVATION OF VIRGINIA ANTIQUITIES.

Address 3215 E Broad Street, Richmond, VA 23223 | Getting there Bus 4A, 4B, 56 to
Marshall & 33rd Streets | Hours Daily dawn−dusk | Tip On the grounds of the Statehouse
is *Mantle* by Mohawk artist Alan Michelson. another monument to the Indigenous people
of Virginia. The design of its spiral walkway was inspired by the pattern on a cloak belonging
to Chief Powhatan, now on display at the Ashmolean Museum in England (1000 Bank
Street, www.alanmichelson.com/mantle).

74 Rest in Pieces
Finding beauty in death

Fittingly situated one block away from Hollywood Cemetery sits "Richmond's premier oddity shop," Rest in Pieces. Except for a mural of the Grim Reaper, the outside is black and austere in amazing contrast to the inside of the shop, which is packed wall-to-wall, floor-to-ceiling with curiosities. The merchandise in the store is diverse, including tarot cards, divination crystals, various flora, and books about entomology, but the most striking feature is the expertly preserved animals greeting you at every turn.

The shelves are saturated with jars of wet specimens like a double-headed pig fetus, acrylic blocks holding scorpions and tarantulas, and all manner of horns and bones. Furry taxidermy creatures ranging in size from a cottontail rabbit to a giraffe rest on the floor and hang from the walls. There are even two human skeletons, Victoria and George. Every one of these creatures comes with its own story, and although everything is dead, the room feels ironically full of life.

To those uninitiated in the preservation of animal bodies, the space seems more like a museum curated by Dr. Moreau than a shop, but to a niche community in Richmond and beyond, these specimens are potential home decor and almost everything has a price tag. There are a few pieces that the owners will not sell, including one of their most iconic specimens - the double-headed calf head (heads?). Equal parts cute and off-putting, the piece encapsulates all that is beautiful and scary about life after death.

Despite the macabre overtones, the owners' intention is to create a welcoming environment for everyone, and they put great effort into making sure all of their pieces are ethically sourced. In this same spirit of community, the shop also hosts classes in various aspects of preservation, such as Atlas Moth pinning and Virginia skull identification.

Address 349 S Laurel Street, Richmond, VA 23220, +1 (804) 649-1666, www.restinpiecesrva.com, riprichmond@gmail.com | **Getting there** Bus 5 to Cary & Laurel Streets | **Hours** Sun 11am–5pm, Mon noon–5pm, Tue–Sat 11am–6pm | **Tip** Check out Rest in Pieces before your reservation around the corner at L'Opossum, and tip your hat to their own taxidermy mascot keeping watch above the bar. Although the food is exquisite, you could easily mistake the restaurant for a sexy, playful, dimly lit funhouse (626 China Street, www.lopossum.com).

75 — Richmond BMX

Real-life Excitebike in Gillie's Creek Park

When ACDC's "Hell's Bells" begins playing over the speakers at Gillie's Creek Park, it's time for the racers to assemble at the back of the hill. Moments later, a recorded voice issues these instructions, "[o]kay riders, random start. Riders ready? Watch the lights," followed by a pregnant pause, and a "beep-beep-beeeeeep, CLANK." With the drop of the gate, the racers begin pedaling furiously down the starting hill.

This is the rapid-fire sequence of events that happens over and over again every Sunday at Gillie's Creek Park, home to the 1050-foot racetrack that serves as the primary venue for Richmond BMX. The track is open for the public to enjoy every day except during scheduled events. On Sundays, riders of all stripes and all ages from two to 72 show up to compete.

At first glance, BMX culture seems intense, rife with complex gear, loud neon jerseys, and heavy metal nicknames. Walking near the track on race days, though, dispels that perception. Each Sunday, a vibrant community of Richmond BMX volunteers, racers, their families, and spectators, categories which overlap significantly, gathers along the fence parallel to the first straightaway, with pop-up tents and grills to break bread and cheer on their racers.

The first event of the race day features the smallest racers on Strider bikes riding on their very own little track tucked in between the lines of the giant cursive "M" that makes up the main track. Spectators will likely also get to watch track legend and Richmond BMX founder, Art Luck, compete in the 56+ cruiser division, along with more racers on this end of the age spectrum. Mr. Luck, now in his 70s, used to compete nationally, and he remains the affable patriarch of the track that he built with his own hands in 1998, with help from other volunteers. "I've been out there so long," he says. "I'm practically part of the track."

Address 4401 Hobbs Lane, Richmond, VA 23231, +1 (804) 397-3781, www.usabmx.com/tracks/1914, richmondbmx@gmail.com | Getting there Bus 4A to Admiral Gravely & Government Roads or bus 56 to Government Road & 1334 | Hours Daily 7am–7pm | Tip In 2015, California-based Stone Brewing Company found its "perfect East Coast home" in Richmond, right across Williamsburg Road from Gillie's Creek Park. After the race, cool down in the tap room here with a Stone IPA (4300 Williamsburg Avenue, www.stonebrewing.com/visit/outposts/richmond).

76 The Richmond Dairy

If these milk bottles could talk…

Few images hearken back to Progressive Era America like the delivery man, dressed in a white suit and hat and black bow tie, walking up to the doorstep with a cheerful wave, a smile, and a crate of glass bottles full of fresh milk. In early 20th century Richmond, the main supplier of moo-juice was the Richmond Dairy Company, purveyors of milk and Dolly Madison ice cream.

The company began in 1890 and in 1913 commissioned its iconic downtown factory, a large brick building buttressed at three corners by 40-foot stonework milk bottles. In the 19th century most milk was delivered in pails or in tin bottles. To promote the superior hygiene of the sterile, sealed glass bottles the dairy company had adopted, they designed the factory as the ultimate advertisement.

The advent of home refrigeration in the '30s spelled the beginning of the end for the Richmond Dairy Company, which closed in 1970. When the building fell into disrepair, it became a commune for struggling artists and musicians. Among those who lived between the milk bottles were members of Death Piggy, which eventually became renowned trash metal monster band GWAR, who recorded their first successful album *Scumbags of the Universe* there.

In a 2015 TedTalk, Michael Bishop, aka Blöthar, former bassist and current lead singer of GWAR since the passing of frontman Dave Brocky, described the importance of the building to the Richmond arts scene in the '80s. "It was a dilapidated, rundown space… full of a bunch of hippies and artists and ne'er-do-wells, punk rockers, and that's where we could afford to put our rehearsal space, where we could afford to create art, to have art studios…. GWAR was born and it would not have happened had it not been for the Richmond Dairy."

In its current incarnation, the space has been renovated into upscale apartments, but the milk bottles remain in place, looking after Jackson Ward.

Address 201 W Marshall Street, Richmond, VA 23220, +1 (804) 788-8888,
www.colonydairy.com | Getting there Bus 3A, 3B, 3C, 14, 50 to Broad & Adams Streets |
Hours Unrestricted from the outside only | Tip Since 1984, the finest dairy in Richmond
has come courtesy of Gelati Celesti, now serving scoops at seven locations across the city
(8906 A West Broad Street, www.gelatiicecream.com).

77 Richmond Fencing Club

Sabre the flavor in Scott's Addition

For those who consider fencing a sport for the aristocracy, confined to ivy-covered boarding schools and royal courtyards, the Richmond Fencing Club (RFC) is here to dispel these notions. "Compared to other sports, it's actually really accessible," says head coach and former Virginia foil champion Cyndi Lucente. At $100 per month for an individual or $160 for a family, which includes access to all classes, a venue for open fencing, and equipment for intro and beginner classes, she has a solid case.

The RFC has existed since the 1960s and moved into its current location in Scott's Addition in 2005. The space consists of two long rooms decorated with international flags strung from the ceiling, framed photographs of RFC legends of yore dotting the cinder block walls, and a long shelf of trophies and medals hanging along the western wall. In the middle, several pairs of fencers in bright white kits and faceless black masks advance and retreat like tango dancers trying to stab each other.

The club currently has about 150 members, ranging in age from 8 to 80 and in skill level from never-held-a-weapon to Olympic hopeful. Lucente says the club is particularly welcoming to kids and draws a wide variety of personalities, including absolute athletes, shy kids who don't like team sports, and intellectual types (fencing is called "physical chess" after all). The sport is universally appealing to their younger members, states Lucente. "You get to hit someone with a sword, and you get celebrated for doing that."

The coaches take fencing seriously, but more important to them is the community they've built. Lucente says, "[w]e're competitive, but we're about making each other successful. My husband and I wanted to make the club feel like family, and I'm more proud of that than any of our results." You are welcome to tour the facility on Tuesdays and Thursdays at 7:30pm.

Address 3411 1/2 Carlton Street, Richmond, VA 23230,+1 (804) 622-3655, www.richmondfencing.com, info@richmondfencing.com | Getting there Bus 20 to Arthur Ashe Boulevard & Moore Street | Hours Tue & Thu 7:30pm – 9pm, see website for class schedule | Tip With its characteristic repurposed warehouses and factories, Scott's Addition is not known for its greenery, but Brambly Park provides a verdant exception to the rule. Two doors down from the RFC, the space serves as a restaurant, winery, park, and music venue (1708 Belleville Street, www.bramblypark.com).

78 Richmond Hill

Historic sanctuary atop Church Hill

Before there was a church on Church Hill, the area was known as Richmond Hill, a term that now refers to the storied cluster of buildings in its westernmost corner. Since their boundaries were set by the city's founder in 1737, the buildings have served as a private home to Richmond's early aristocrats and enslaved servants, a Catholic monastery, and now a spiritual retreat center. They retain elements from each era of their long history.

The consortium of churches that now owns the site welcomes the public for short, impromptu visits or longer, scheduled retreats. If you come here seeking sanctuary, you'll find no shortage of places to sit and reflect. But along the journey, you'll also find subtle reminders of Richmond's painful past, wounds that the spiritual community there address every morning in a prayer for the city.

Head first for the cupola atop the Adams-Taylor house, accessed by a series of stairways emptying into a tiny, bright, warm room with the best view in the city. A plaque there recalls the summer of 1862, when a boy living on premises sat in the cupola with a spyglass watching smoke 10 miles north of Richmond as it migrated eastward over the course of a week, an event now known as the Seven Days Battle. From the cupola, you can walk to the dome-ceilinged chapel, a peaceful space usually lit only by sun refracted through stained glass. The clergy in residence meet there three times daily for prayer.

From the chapel, walk behind the buildings into a remarkable garden in the heart of the city but hidden behind ancient brick walls. Meandering along the winding walkway, you'll pass the plants cultivated lovingly by the sisters of the Catholic monastery, and you'll see the excavated dwelling that once housed enslaved people. Have a seat on a bench, gaze upon the city, and reflect on its struggles and prosperity, past and present.

Address 2209 E Grace Street, Richmond, VA 23223, +1 (804) 783-7903,
www.richmondhillva.org, info@richmondhillva.org | Getting there BRT Bus to Shockoe
Bottom Eastbound Station | Hours Tue–Sat 9am–5pm, Sun 9am–4pm | Tip When you're
done reflecting in the garden, go around the corner and pick up some pie – one savory, like
the curried lamb & spinach, and one sweet, like the buttermilk & raspberry – from the
Kiwis at Proper Pie (2505 E Broad Street, No. 100, www.properpieco.com).

79 Richmond Pinball Collective

Hit the flippers with the pinheads of Midlothian

Part arcade, part nonprofit, part social club, the Richmond Pinball Collective's (RPC) core purpose is, per their website, to "spread the joy of pinball to the people." Good nights to swing by are when the Flip Side, the RPC's resident league, hosts its well-attended biweekly competition or the monthly gathering of the Belles and Chimes, the collective's all-female league. On those special nights, the backboxes are lit, the bumpers are popping, and there's an energy in the air not evident from the outside if you're looking at the nondescript strip mall off the Midlothian Turnpike.

The space holds between 25 and 30 machines that span the chronology of pinball history, from classics like 1979's Gorgar to the Foo Fighters game that was released in 2023. The best part of the collective? No quarters required. There's a certain joy that one gets from pushing the start button on a pinball machine without first having to drop in some coins. There's probably a word for that feeling in another language, like *flipperfreude*, but English-speakers have yet to coin an appropriate term for this complex emotion.

The collective was started in 2017 by husband and wife Clark and Laura Fraley, pinball enthusiasts seeking to form a community around their shared affinity for the silver ball. The space looks like a typical arcade, but full of warmth and camaraderie. Members reinforce that the group embraces all skill levels, so don't despair when you drain three balls in 30 seconds on Demolition Man. Guests may drop in up to three times a year for $15/ visit, but the real value comes with an affordable monthly or six-month membership offered for individuals and families. Truly all are welcome at the Richmond Pinball Collective, so pull the plunger and soak in that sweet, sweet *flipperfreude*.

Address 9550 Midlothian Turnpike, No. 106, Richmond, VA 23235, +1 (804) 544-1252, www.richmondpinballcollective.com | Getting there Bus 1A to Midlothian Turnpike & Moorefield Park Drive | Hours Mon 6–10pm, Tue 11am–2pm, Wed & Thu 6–10pm, Fri 11am–2pm, Sat 1–7pm | Tip With a solid lineup of scary-movie themed pinball machines, Wax Moon spreads the horror of pinball to the people. Primarily a record store, the shop welcomes the public to open-play pinball with no time limit for $10 (1310 Altamont Avenue, www.waxmoonrecords.com).

80 Richmond Raceway Infield

A quiet walk around the region's biggest venue

It's surreal to stand in the infield of an empty Richmond Raceway surrounded by 51,000 vacant seats, considering that over 112,000 people - just under half the population of Richmond proper - have attended at past races. On a handful of non-race weekends though, when the track is only open for the Richard Petty Driving Experience, the stands are completely empty, as is the infield, save for a few dozen participants.

On those days, anyone is welcome to drive in through the vehicle tunnel under turn 3 and walk around the FanGrounds. Highlights of the infield complex include the NASCAR Cup Series garage, where the cars line up awaiting warm-up laps. Walking toward turn 1 between the garage and pit road, you will notice that the ground suddenly turns to the black and white checkerboard of Victory Lane, where racing legends have sat or stood on the driver window, littered in confetti and splashing fans with whatever drink sponsors their cars.

For race fans, these are sacred grounds, dating back to the origins of stock car racing in the US. The first auto race here was held in 1946, and the first race on the precursor to the NASCAR circuit occurred in 1953, making it the fourth oldest track still in use. Speaking of Richard Petty, "the King" remains royalty at Richmond, holding a record 12 wins on the track. His father Lee won the first ever NASCAR race there held in 1953, and his son Kyle won in 1986.

Empty though the stands may be, kids will be delighted to see (and hear) the handful of race cars lined up in the pits and ripping around track at race day speeds. Watching from the infield is free, but if you're willing to spring for a ride along or a drive, the ultimate vantage of the track is from inside one of these vehicles, glued to your seat by G-forces. For River City motorheads, a drive into the infield is an unforgettable experience.

Address 600 E Laburnum Avenue, Richmond, VA 23222, +1 (866) 455-7223, www.richmondraceway.com | Getting there Bus 91 to E Laburnum Avenue & Meadowbridge Road | Hours See website for event schedule | Tip If you're not quite ready for the big track, warm up on the go-karts at Windy Hill in Midlothian (16500 Midlothian Turnpike, Midlothian, www.windyhillsports.com/go-karts).

81 Richmond Railroad Museum

Honoring the city's roots in the rails

Richmond has a special relationship with trains. The five railroads that intersected the city in the middle of the 19th century made it attractive as a strategic capital during the Civil War. In the 1880s, Richmond began operating the world's first citywide, electric trolley system. From the Triple Crossing, to Main Street Station, to the CSX bridge spanning the James River, Richmond's railroad infrastructure is among the city's most iconic landmarks. The quintessential Richmond cityscape would have to include a freight train chugging along the James on the C&O railroad.

To celebrate Virginia's love of locomotives, the Old Dominion chapter of the National Railway Historical Society operates the Richmond Railroad Museum in Manchester. Set inside the renovated Hull Street Station, a stop on the passenger line of the Southern Railway from 1915 to 1957, the building itself is a piece of railway history. The Station Master's Office is an authentic relic of the original building. In the large Freight Room, the museum displays historical artifacts highlighting the railroad industry in Central Virginia over the last two centuries. Out back, kids can climb into the engine of a 1924 steam locomotive and the caboose of a 1969 Seaboard Coastline boxcar.

The highlight of the museum is the city's largest model train display. Watch intently as little locomotives shoot through the Blue Ridge Mountains, traverse bridges over the James, and wind between the iconic buildings in downtown Richmond. There's even a button that makes a tiny Patrick Henry (1736–1799) deliver the lines that launched the Revolutionary War, while a choo-choo rolls by anachronistically. On Saturdays and Sundays, the stewards of the museum, a community of mostly older gents, are on hand and very happy to share their encyclopedic knowledge about trains and the city that loves them.

Address 102 Hull Street, Richmond, VA 23224, +1 (804) 231-4324, www.richmondrailroadmuseum.com, info@richmondrailroadmuseum.com | Getting there Bus 1A, 1B, 1C to Hull & 3rd Streets | Hours Sat 11am–4pm, Sun 1–4pm | Tip Train enthusiasts must not miss the triple crossing in downtown, one of two places in North America where three Class I railroads cross over one another (1401 Dock Street).

82 Richmond Triangle Players

Trailblazers among the city's theater community

Even if you didn't know what goes on within the Robert B. Moss Theater, you'd likely notice the large, multicolored triangles along the exterior. "Something gay is happening here," you'll deduce. Indeed the building provides a colorful, well-appointed home to the Richmond Triangle Players (RTP), the mid-Atlantic's premier outlet for LGBT-QIA+-oriented theater. But it wasn't always so.

Amid the socially conservative atmosphere of the early 1990s, before safe spaces for the gay and lesbian community had enough real estate in Richmond to facilitate a culture, a collection of talented individuals found sanctuary upstairs at Fielden's, a members-only, gay nightclub on West Broad. Early attendees of RTP performances fondly recall the space as "small," "sketchy," and smelling of beer, but it was there that Richmond's gay theater scene was born.

RTP's founders were all-in on LGBTQIA+ themes and causes from the get-go, with a debut performance on November 4, 1992 of three one-act Harvey Fierstein plays called the *Safe Sex Trilogy*, the proceeds of which went to the Richmond AIDS Information Network. The success of these performances propelled the group toward its first formal season the following year, including a production of the subtly titled *Vampire Lesbians from Sodom*. The company never looked back, producing over 150 plays and several world premieres over its 30 years.

In 2010, RTP bought a former radiator shop in Scott's Addition and opened the Moss Theater. Since 1992, the city has evolved, and attitudes nationally toward the LGBTQIA+ community have softened, but the importance of RTP to its community does not feel diminished. From the welcoming nature of the ushers to the cocktail-party vibe at intermission, you get a sense that the mission of the institution is much more than putting on good theater.

Address 1300 Altamont Avenue, Richmond, VA 23230, +1 (804)-346-8113, www.rtriangle.org | Getting there Bus 50 to Broad Street & Belmont Avenue | Hours See website for show schedule | Tip Among local theater groups, the Virginia Repertory Theatre claims the largest (553 seats) and oldest (circa 1911) stage space with the November Theatre. Several notable actors have called the theater home, including Frank Morgan, the original Wizard of Oz (114 W Broad Street, www.va-rep.org/november.html).

83 River City Roller Derby

I gotta have more cowbell, baby!

When the green cowbells are clanging at the Rollerdome, Richmond's fiercest skaters, those gritty, glittery warriors belonging to the River City Roller Derby (RCRD), are battling for glory on the flat track. The hometown league was founded in 2006 as the River City Rollergirls and rebranded as the more inclusive RCRD in 2017 to accommodate a greater diversity of gender identities. As Richmond's roller derby community has become more diverse, it's also grown larger. It has now split into two teams for monthly home scrimmages: Poe's Punishers and the Hollywood Undertakers.

The RCRD's public relations rep Chattahoochee, aka Hoochie, swears the competition is not as fierce as people think. But the contact inside the scrum that gradually orbits the track like a moon made of humans says otherwise, as does a vicious hip check that sends a jammer pinwheeling out of bounds. "Some leagues play for fun, some for rankings; we play for community," Hoochie says. "Different people view the sport differently though. It's evolved into more of a skill sport, but we have some hard hitters that hearken back to the good ole days of derby - skaters that are not *not* proud of the time they spend in the penalty box."

The rituals of RCRD skater development contribute to the sense of community as new recruits metamorphosize into battle-hardened vets. Intense, 12-week orientations are held twice a year, at the end of which skaters must pass a rigorous skills test in order to compete. Having passed the test, a skater is then ceremoniously bestowed with their skater name, a process that has provided such gems on the current roster as Cindy Boo Hoo, Betty Clocker, Princess Die, Punky Bruiser, Slaying Mantis, Pippi StrongBlocking, PeeWee HurtsMen, Tonya Farting, and the RVA-centric Cannibelle Lee. When you've got a fever, the only prescription is more cowbell at the Rollerdome!

Address 4902 Williamsburg Road, Richmond, VA 23231, www.rivercityrollerderby.com, rivercityrollerderby@gmail.com | **Getting there** Bus 7B, 56 to Williamsburg & Robins Roads | **Hours** See website for schedule | **Tip** Trade the grit for grace and go see the River City Magnolias, Richmond's amateur water ballet team, who schedule several public performances throughout the year. During the warm months, they rotate among six different pools within the Richmond public parks system, and in colder months, they use the Swansboro indoor pool in Midlothian (3160 Midlothian Turnpike, www.facebook.com/RiverCityMagnolias).

84 Robins Nature Center

A birds-eye view of Virginia nature

When it comes to enjoying the abundance of Virginia's nature, there's no substitute for a hike in the Blue Ridge Mountains or a paddle on the Chesapeake Bay. Even within Richmond city limits, the James River and a multitude of trails provide easy access to the great outdoors. For all you indoorsy types or those with small children on a rainy day, though, the Robins Center at Maymont has distilled the magic of Virginia's ecology into 30,000 gallons worth of aquaria within a 29,000-square-foot structure.

Run of the River, the main attraction of the center, originates at the roaring waterfall that greets visitors at the entrance to the exhibit room. From there, the stream flows into a series of pools representing different sections of the river. Hosted within the tanks is a variety of native Virginian aquatic fauna, including 17 species of fish, blue crabs, seven species of turtle, and at the end, the stars of the show: Louis and Nola, the river otters.

Opposite the aquatic creatures is another series of terraria holding native species of reptiles and amphibians, including two small American alligators named Apex and Sobek; Jafar the northern cottonmouth; Milhouse the northern copperhead; Lucky the timber rattlesnake; and Carl the eastern black rat snake. Look for several species of frogs and salamanders as well. The best vantage from which to take it all in is atop River Reach, the 34-foot-tall climbing tower right in the middle. Encased in wire netting, the tower provides kids a safe place to climb up to an eagle-eye view of the entire center.

The Nature Center is one of three programs at Maymont displaying animals, alongside the Maymont Farm, which hosts cows, horses, goats, sheep, pigs, ducks, chickens, and a Sicilian donkey; and the enclosures that hold native Virginia wildlife, including black bears, bison, bobcats, foxes, and birds of prey.

Address 2201 Shields Lake Drive, Richmond, VA 23220, +1 (804) 525-9000, https://maymont.org/what-to-see/nature-center | Getting there Bus 78 to Meadow Street & Colorado Avenue | Hours See website for seasonal hours | Tip While at Maymont, visit the ornately furnished mansion there owned by James and Alice Dooley. The object that best symbolizes their decadence is an impressive bed in the shape of a giant swan (1700 Hampton Street, https://maymont.org/mansion).

85 Ruins at Belle Isle

Architectural ghosts on the James

On Belle Isle, dappled sunlight shines onto the shoulders of joggers. The broad rocks of its banks host sunbathing turtles and truant teenagers alike. Rapids carrying rafts roar past herons stabbing pointy beaks at American shad. Amid the vim and vigor of life on this jewel of the James, though, stands a host of ruins, somber storytellers speaking on behalf of the individuals who have toiled and died here over the centuries.

When one speaks of "the ruins of Belle Isle," some specificity is needed, as this may refer to any of several abandoned structures littered across its 54 acres. Looking east from the catwalk suspended above the river, you'll see the crumbling stumps of a c. 1870 railroad bridge leading to the rusted-out skeleton of the "the Chrysler building," the former warehouse where the hatches of Chrysler-branded tanks were constructed during World War I. For the audacious, the eerie, graffitied shell of the 1905 Belle Isle Hydroelectric Plant sits on the southern bank of the island.

Dating to 1814, the oldest ruin on the island is the faded, vine-covered brick façade of the Belle Isle Iron & Nail Works. Indentured Europeans and enslaved Black laborers once walked through its beautiful arched doorways into a massive manufactory to forge nails, wire, and horseshoes from scrap iron pulled into the facility by mule. The building also bore witness to one of the South's most infamous prisoner-of-war camps, rudimentary structures where thousands of Union soldiers perished under abysmal conditions.

Nowadays, the archway transports visitors from one wooded doorstep into an even larger, emptier expanse of woods, its bricks bleeding a chilly dampness as though one were walking through the body of a wraith. The idyllic surroundings provide a perfect setting to lose yourself in the present, but the buildings are there to remind you about the past, lest ye forget.

Address 344 Tredegar Street, Richmond, VA 23219, +1 (804) 646-8911, www.jamesriverpark.org/explore-the-park-belle-isle | Getting there Bus 87 to Second Street & Brown's Island Way or bus 3A, 3B, 3C to Belvedere & Holly Streets | Hours Daily dawn–dusk | Tip If grandpappy's hooch is making you blind, instead visit the tasting room at Belle Isle Craft Spirits to sip on the area's finest (above-board) moonshine (615 Maury Street, www.belleislecraftspirits.com).

86 _Rumors of War_
A new rider in the Museum District

On December 10, 2019, a bronze statue of a man on horseback was unveiled on the lawn of the VMFA. The pose of his horse and the large, granite pedestal on which he rode were strikingly similar to three other statues in the neighborhood, namely the trio of Confederate generals that had stood in place along Monument Avenue since 1890, 1907, and 1917. The statue felt different, though, for the features of its rider, a young, dreadlocked, Black man bedecked in a hoodie, ripped jeans, and Air Jordans. By September 2021, less than two years after its arrival, _Rumors of War_ stood alone as the only figure looming over the Fan & Museum Districts on horseback.

The VMFA hosted an exhibit in 2016 called _Kehinde Wiley: A New Republic_ and welcomed the artist to Richmond for its opening. While in town, Wiley strolled along Monument Avenue and contemplated what the statues there meant to the city's residents. According to the VMFA website, Wiley later said this about the origins of _Rumors of War_: "[i]n these toxic times art can help us transform and give us a sense of purpose. This story begins with my seeing the Confederate monuments. What does it feel like if you are black and walking beneath this? We come from a beautiful, fractured situation. Let's take these fractured pieces and put them back together."

In 2020, the Richmond city government decided to remove the Confederate monuments, settling a long-smoldering local controversy with national repercussions and turning the page on the city's long love affair with Lost Cause mythology. Though the statues have come down, _Rumors of War_ stands within a stone's throw of other extant Confederate landmarks. Notably, the sculpture faces the temple-like headquarters of the United Daughters of the Confederacy, an organization whose published mission statement includes "Honoring the memory of its Confederate ancestors."

RUMORS OF WAR

KEHINDE WILEY
2019

Address 200 N Arthur Ashe Boulevard, Richmond, VA 23220, +1 (804) 340-1400, www.vmfa.museum | Getting there Bus 20 to Robinson Street & Hanover Avenue or bus 77 to Grove Avenue & N Arthur Ashe Boulevard | Hours Sat–Tue 10am–5pm, Wed–Fri 10am–9pm | Tip Another notable outdoor sculpture is *The Headman*, a bronze statue on Brown's Island honoring the contributions of the Black boat operators who ran the city's early commerce on the Kanawha Canal. The statue lends its silhouette to the Richmond city flag (Brown's Island, South 7th Street, www.bateaurva.com/history-the-headman).

87 — Scuffletown Park
Flourishing Fan pocket park

Richmond does an excellent job of preserving its natural beauty, and the densely populated Fan neighborhood is no exception. It's dotted with pocket parks like Federal, Sydney, Meadow, and Paradise Parks, and citizens team up to bring nature back between the concrete slabs. One such setting is Scuffletown Park, a tiny urban oasis abloom, bordered by the townhouses of Strawberry Street and Stuart, Stafford, and Park Avenues.

The origin of the park's name is a matter of debate, but by the 1790s, the neighborhood around the park became known as Scuffle Towne, possibly related to a dust-up between American militiamen and British troops during Benedict Arnold's Raid on Richmond in 1781. The moniker also lent itself to the local thoroughfare, Old Scuffletown Road (now Park Avenue) and the Scuffletown Tavern, a drinking establishment that sat at the corner of Park & Strawberry from 1792–1910.

In 1974, the city officially designated the land a park and hired Williamsburg architect Carlton Abbott to design it and its sibling Paradise Park. In 1999, the Fan District Association spearheaded a renovation, replacing most of the concrete, geometric features that had become popular with skateboarders and graffiti artists, with green spaces.

These days, a group of organized volunteers called Friends of Scuffletown Park are responsible for its upkeep, and they do a marvelous job cultivating a flourishing garden, keeping the seating areas clean, and manicuring the lawn. Accessible through two trellises covered in China roses, the garden portion houses a diverse array of flowers, with increasing attention paid to nourishing the Fan's native pollinators. No two visits here are the same, with an ever-changing lineup of flora, each taking their turn through the procession of the seasons to the delight of picnickers, strollers, and sunbathers in this tucked-in city sanctuary.

Address 418 Strawberry Street, Richmond, VA 23220 | Getting there Bus 20 to Robinson Street & Kensington Avenue | Hours Daily 7am–8pm | Tip The perfect grub for your picnic at Scuffletown is a pizza from 8 ½, located at the end of the alley leading into the park (401 Strawberry Street, www.eightandahalfrva.com).

88   Section O

Home to the River City Red Army

Decades before an affable Kansan by the name of Ted Lasso took the helm at AFC Richmond, another Richmond football club was dominating the pitch. Founded in 1993, the Richmond Kickers are the oldest continuously operating professional soccer club in the US. Over the years, the club has won regular season championships in tiers two, three, and four in the ever-evolving American soccer hierarchy. In 1995, the Kickers won the US Open Cup and remain the only club outside of the top two tiers etched onto the base of the hallowed Dewar Cup.

Richmond has traditionally had a difficult time holding onto its sports franchises. Since the arrival of the Kickers, the city has waved goodbye to the Rage (women's professional basketball); Braves (minor league baseball); Renegades and RiverDogs (minor league hockey); and Raiders, Revolution, and Roughriders (arena football). The Kickers have been a stable presence in an otherwise turbulent market.

Since 2010, the club's main supporters group has been the River City Red Army, an outfit of flag-waving, drumbeating, face-painted hooligans chanting through the red smoke of Section O at City Stadium on matchday. From mid-March to mid-October, the Kickers welcome the Red Army and fans more broadly to matches, generally held on Saturday evenings at City Stadium, a vintage arena dating to 1929 and home of the Kickers since 1995.

Despite the militaristic moniker, the Red Army bills itself as "a friendly bunch," and welcomes with open arms Kickers supporters of all stripes to tailgates starting three hours before matches. You can't beat a warm summer night at City Stadium, with a wide-open, pink and yellow skyscape, a cold beer, and the ruckus from section O as the Red Army cries out:

Oh when I go [Oh when I go] / Oh when I go they'll bury me in Section O / And when I'm dead [And when I'm dead] / And when I'm dead they'll bury me in Kickers red.

Address 3201 Maplewood Avenue, Richmond, VA 23221, +1 (804) 644-5425, www.rivercityredarmy.org, rivercityredarmy@gmail.com | Getting there Bus 20 to Freeman Road & Maplewood Avenue | Hours Check website for schedule | Tip Kickers legend Bobby Ukrop, who scored in the club's US Open championship game in 1995, is a member of the Ukrop's grocery store dynasty. Today, Ukrop's Market Hall still sells their legendary rainbow cookies, white house rolls, fried chicken, and all the other prepared-food staples (7250 Patterson Avenue, https://ukropshomestylefoods.com/ukrops-market-hall).

89 Sharp's Island
Wilderness in the center of the city

The effect that the wilderness has on a world-weary, modern human, or the perception of solidarity with the natural world and separation from the artificial one, is generally reserved for settings far away from cities. In Richmond, however, that isolation is available with just a short canoe paddle from Manchester over to Sharp's Island, a tiny, teardrop-shaped isle in the stretch of the James running through downtown.

The island is the only place within city limits where you can legally camp, and for $65, you get it all to yourself for an evening to play castaway under a canopy of trees, buffered by the roar of the James, with only the insects and great blue herons keeping company. No structures are allowed on the island, although a modest outhouse labeled "Takeout #2," made the cut, as did the camping platforms. An old Richmond Times-Dispatch newspaper box has been converted into a Little Free Library, befittingly containing a copy of *Treasure Island.*

The only permanent resident of the island is *Edwards the Fisherman*, a sculpture made of rusty tool parts welded together by artist Keith Ramsey. Edwards stands atop the ruins of a brick house dating from 1895, owned by the Sharp family that gave the island its name. Everyone else, campers and herons alike, are just transients.

The sound of the rapids drown out the car traffic over the Mayo Bridge just 300 feet to the East but are no match for the railcars that periodically thunder over the Norfolk Southern train bridge to the west. Just beyond the rapids to the North, peeking out from above the Mayo Island tree line, are the skyscrapers that comprise the city skyline. The Manchester flood wall and giant grain silos of the abandoned Southern States factory predominate the view to the South. Despite urban elements nearby in every direction, the city nevertheless feels remarkably far away.

Address Parking lot for Floodwall Park at 101 Hull Street, Richmond, VA 23224, www.hipcamp.com/en-US/land/virginia-sharp-s-island-v1qh0lpp?adults=1&children=0 | **Getting there** Bus 1A to Hull & 3rd Streets, then walk to the south bank of the river. The island is only accessible by boat. | **Hours** By reservation only | **Tip** Just north of Sharp's Island, you'll find Brown's Island, one of the best outdoor venues in the city for music, including the Friday Cheers summer concert series (S 7th Street, www.brownsisland.com).

90 Shockoe Sessions Live

Acoustic sanctuary in the heart of downtown

Nothing beats live music. Take a sterile, polished studio song, blend in expanded solos, broken guitar strings, and mic feedback, soak it in the sweaty elixir of a live venue, and watch a complex creature replete with flaws and flourishes come to life. All too often, though, this magical process comes at the expense of good sound, and fans leave the show with their ears bleeding. Live music with studio quality acoustics is indeed an elusive creature, but Richmonders can catch a glimpse every Tuesday night, thanks to the Shockoe Sessions Live.

Hosted by Shockoe Records and In Your Ear Studio, the sessions feature a local artist playing to an audience of about 30 people. The studio is an immaculate space in a 19th century, brick building in the heart of Shockoe Bottom. To get to the show, you will walk past framed platinum records and photographs of the myriad artists who have performed here, through soundproof metal doors, and finally into the inner sanctuary of Studio A.

The space just feels good. It smells nice, the temperature is just right, and the lighting is soothing. It's large enough to accommodate an audience but small enough to feel intimate, and there's a mellow dog named Rosie wearing a Shockoe Records t-shirt. Most importantly, the walls soak up unwanted reverb to produce an incredibly pure sound from the band at the front of the room.

The studio has hosted over 200 sessions, all featuring artists from Virginia and most from Richmond. The events started around 2012 but were only held quarterly until the spring of 2020, when In Your Ear owner Carlos Chafin began hosting live-streamed concerts on a weekly basis with musicians sidelined from touring due to the COVID-19 pandemic. In 2022, the series began welcoming a live audience of lucky Richmonders and never stopped. Come hear for yourself, but be forewarned: it may ruin live music for you.

Address 1813 East Broad Street, Richmond, VA 23223, www.shockoesessionslive.com, reese@shockoerecords.com | Getting there Bus 7A, 7B, 56 to Broad & 19th Streets | Hours See website for performance schedule | Tip The WRBX-RVA Boombox also hosts recorded sessions before a live audience, though in a slightly different setting: a repurposed shipping container. Their sessions welcome music of all genres but focus primarily on hip-hop (6 West Cary Street, www.rvaboombox.com).

91 Shrine of Memory

Monument to Virginia's fallen heroes

One of the best views in the city can be found atop Gamble's Hill from within the Shrine of Memory, an open-air, rectangular structure whose eastern façade is a giant glass window, 35-feet tall and 145-feet long. In the foreground, a green lawn slopes down to Tredegar, Brown's Island, and the James. Skyscrapers forming the city skyline drop off at the Manchester Bridge in the background. The exceptional view is enhanced by etchings in the glass of the names of the 10,000 Virginians who gave their lives in the service of their country during World War II.

In 1950, the Virginia General Assembly authorized the placement of a memorial to the Virginians killed in combat during the Second World War. Between its design and dedication, several hundred more Virginians died in the Korean War, and their names were added to the interior of the western wall, later to be joined by those who perished in Vietnam, the Persian Gulf, and in 21st century conflicts. Altogether, nearly 12,000 names are listed on the walls. At the southern end of the tunnel, these individuals are mourned by *Memory*, a 23-foot-tall, white marble statue of a grieving woman watching over an eternal flame that burns at her feet.

The Shrine of Memory was the original structure of what has now become the Virginia War Memorial, a complex featuring an 18,000-square-foot museum, a lecture hall, library, and a 250-seat amphitheater. The museum has permanent displays dedicated to the participation of Virginians in every American conflict dating to the Revolutionary War and rotating exhibit space displaying the art of veterans from the Commonwealth. Those interior spaces are worth visiting, but the original memorial, with its views of the city, remains the heart of the complex. Visitors can gaze upon the splendors of the city and appreciate the sacrifices of the men and women who served.

Address 621 S Belvidere Street, Richmond, VA 23220, +1 (804) 786-2060, www.vawarmemorial.org, info@vawarmemorial.org | Getting there Bus 3A, 3B, 3C to Belvedere Street & VA War Memorial | Hours Mon–Sat 9am–4pm, Sun noon–4pm | Tip Fort Gregg-Adams outside of Petersburg is home to the US Army Women's Museum, "the only museum in the world dedicated to women in the Army," telling their stories through exhibitions, events, and education (2100 Adams Avenue, Fort Gregg-Adams, https://awm. army.mil).

92 Soldiers' Section

A memorial to Jewish Confederates

Outside of the State of Israel, there are only two Jewish military burial grounds: Weißensee Cemetery in Germany for 395 soldiers who died during World War I and the Soldiers' Section of the Hebrew Cemetery in Shockoe Hill for 30 men who died fighting for the Confederacy during the American Civil War. The Hebrew Cemetery opened in 1817 to replace the still-standing Franklin Street Burying Grounds founded in 1791, and the Soldiers' Section was completed in 1866.

The origin of the Soldiers' Section is a matter of debate, but one source claims that two Confederate military cemeteries at Spotsylvania Court House and Fredericksburg, both near major Civil War battle sites, refused to accept Jewish casualties. So the Hebrew Ladies' Memorial Association took responsibility for the Jewish casualties of those battles near Richmond.

The ladies fundraised and commissioned William Barksdale Myers (1833–1873) to design the central feature of the memorial, an elaborate, wrought-iron fence enclosing it. Each of the fence posts is composed of five muskets leaning against one another, draped with a furled Confederate flag and topped with a forage cap worn by the Infantry. Between the posts, decorative sabers are crossed to honor the cavalry. In the center of the plot, a plaque reads, "To the glory of God and in memory of the Hebrew Confederate soldiers resting in this hallowed spot."

As with other Confederate memorials in Richmond, there is complexity in deciphering the purpose of this site – the balance in honoring the individuals without glorifying their cause. The Soldiers' Section is particularly interesting in that regard because its very existence was born of discrimination against these soldiers, who fought to defend the institution of enslavement, which impacted the ancestors of the people now living beside it in the predominantly Black neighborhood of Gilpin Court.

Address 400 Hospital Street, Richmond, VA 23219, +1 (804) 353-2668,
www.bethahabah.org/heritage/hebrew-cemetery, bama@bethahabah.org | Getting there
Bus 3A, 3B, 3C to 5th & Hospital Streets | Hours Sun–Fri 8am–4pm | Tip Just across
the street in Shockoe Cemetery is the grave of Elizabeth van Lew, Richmond socialite,
abolitionist, and leader of a Union spy ring. A moving epitaph about her sacrifice in pursuit
of abolition is on her gravestone. The graves of Chief Justice John Marshall and Edgar Allan
Poe's sweetheart Elmira Royster are nearby (320 Hospital Street).

93 Squashapenny Junction

Shop in the store that time forgot

There are rules at Squashapenny Junction, an antique store in Doswell set in a white clapboard house packed floor-to-ceiling with all manner of treasures. The rules are born out of practicality and nostalgia for a time before technology ruled your every waking moment. If you keep an open mind and play by them, a good time is in store.

Rule No. 1: Use of cell phones inside the store is not allowed. If you need to use your phone, the owner politely asks that you step out front. The enjoyable outcome of this is that there aren't many pictures of the interior online, so you cannot adequately anticipate the funhouse that lies inside.

Rule No. 2: Make an appointment. The store is so packed with antiquated wonders, and the walkway between them is so narrow that it cannot accommodate more than one party at a time. So you have to plan ahead for your visit. This requirement might seem like an issue given that the store is only open two days a week, but the owner makes it work. You and three friends can drop in and pay $10 each, which is waived if you spend $20.

Rule No. 3: You have one full hour to explore, which is the perfect amount of time to browse in one long loop and then circle back for a second targeted mission. The friendly owner is there to help as needed but otherwise leaves her guests alone. She simply hands you a flashlight at the door to look into some of the darker display cases and then checks in every 15 minutes or so to see if you have questions. When the hour is up, make your purchases or pay your $10.

In a world where most businesses depend on social media exposure for survival, Squashapenny's rejection of technology has created the type of unique experience that keeps appointments booked. The owner acknowledges that the unique format is not for everyone. "Friends tell me the online reviews are mixed," she says. "I don't have a phone, so I don't know."

Address 10570 Doswell Road, Doswell, VA 23047, +1 (804) 876-3083 | Getting there By car, take I-95 to exit 98, turn right onto SR-30 then left onto Doswell Road | Hours Sat & Sun 11am–5pm by appointment only | Tip Another fun shop specializing in pre-loved goods, both modern and vintage, is Class and Trash. Cell phones are welcome, and no appointment is necessary (1720 Altamont Avenue, www.classandtrash.com).

94   Sunken Barges at Dutch Gap
Paddle between the ghost ships

Just after dawn on a crisp November day, a blinding, orange sliver of sun peaks above a maple-lined horizon, silhouetting the broad wing-span of a blue heron as it cuts through billowy vapors steaming off the chilly water at Dutch Gap. Tucked in just south of where the Citie of Henricus once stood lies an 850-acre lagoon hosting a magnificent ecosystem. Home to beavers, muskrats, turtles, frogs, and hundreds of species of birds, the area is a destination for nature lovers.

One species not commonly encountered on ambles around the secluded, 3.5-mile trail encircling the lagoon is the *homo sapien*, although people have been visiting the area for a long time. Ancient Native American artifacts have been unearthed all around the banks of the lagoon. In 1613, Sir Thomas Dale attempted to cut a trench through the massive oxbow in the river to fortify Henricus from Indian attack. Union troops expanded these efforts by forcing freed-men to dig a channel that would circumvent Confederate defenses. In the early 1920s, the Richmond Sand & Gravel Company began mining in the area. This continued until the 1960s, at which point a channel was cut and the river filled the enormous mining pit.

To paddle a 2.5-mile trail through the lagoon, you may portage your own craft from the parking lot at Henricus about 440 yards to the put-in a mile upstream. In the warmer months, kayak and canoe classes leave from the much closer boatshed.

One highlight of the water trail is the Graveyard, a collection of abandoned mining barges that now form a series of islands dense with vegetation. In the middle of the archipelago sits an iconic, rusty, old tugboat sporting a "D" on the smokestack. Although humans have permanently changed the topography at Dutch Gap, nature has reclaimed the sunken fleet at its center.

Address 341 Henricus Park Road, Chester, VA 23836, +1 (804) 748-1624, www.chesterfield.gov/DutchGap | Getting there By car, take I–95 South to exit 61A onto SR-10 East then turn left onto Old Stage Road, right onto Coxendale Road, and right onto Henricus Park Road | Hours Daily 8am–dusk | Tip The Bellwood Flea Market, Richmond's oldest and largest, sets up just up the highway from Henricus. A bustling smorgasbord of goods and produce open on weekend days, the market has particular significance to the Latin communities of the Southside (9201 Jefferson Davis Highway, www.facebook.com/officialbellwoodfleamarket).

95 Tad Lincoln's Flag

A souvenir of surrender

On April 4, 1865, two days after Union forces captured Richmond, President Lincoln and his son Thomas "Tad" Lincoln (1853–1871) visited the ruins of the city, famously stepping onto the banks of the James River to cheers from Union soldiers and newly emancipated Black citizens. The day of their visit was the boy's 12th birthday, and it is believed that on that day, he received a tattered Confederate flag as a birthday present. The circumstances of the flag's provenance are unknown, and it is also a matter of debate whether this was the specific flag that Tad was known to hang outside of his window at the White House.

The flag is now displayed at the American Civil War Museum at Historic Tredegar, a collection of buildings once comprising the factory that supplied the Confederacy with approximately half of its munitions used in battle. After stepping through the ruins of a brick archway and then through the modern glass doors of the museum's entrance, you'll find the 20-foot brick wall that formerly belonged to the Old Foundry. In a building filled with an incredible array of Civil War artifacts, including the aforementioned flag, the saddle on which Robert E. Lee rode to Appomattox, and the suit in which Jefferson Davis was captured, the museum's most amazing artifact may be the structure that contains it.

Another experience at the museum that must not be missed is viewing the award-winning short film *A People's Contest: Struggles for Nation & Freedom in Civil War America*, playing at the theater beyond the Old Foundry wall. By the end of the film, you'll realize how pivotal Richmond, and indeed the very building in which you sit, was to the country's greatest existential crisis. The film is also the perfect primer for the rest of the museum, which provides a diverse narrative from the viewpoints of stakeholders of all stripes: men and women, free and enslaved, Union and Confederate.

Address 480 Tredegar Street, Richmond, VA 23219, +1 (804) 649-1861 x100,
www.acwm.org/historic-tredegar | Getting there Bus 87 to 2nd Street & Brown's Island
Way | Hours Daily 10am–5pm | Tip After getting your share of history inside, step across
the road to the T. Tyler Potterfield Bridge, a 1,700-foot pedestrian walkway across the James.
At the north bank entrance, you'll find an installation called *3 days in April 1865*, explaining
the Confederate evacuation, the Union arrival, and Emancipation Day in Richmond
(access from Brown's Island at the northern end and Semmes Avenue at the south end,
www.jamesriverpark.org/t-tyler-potterfield-memorial-bridge).

96 Tanglewood Ordinary

Pull up a chair for Grandmother's Sunday Dinner

On River Road West, between Crozier and Maidens, sits a log cabin that obstinately defies the passage of time. No matter what is happening beyond the hand-cut poplar timber walls of Tanglewood Ordinary, visitors will find it easy to leave the outside world behind for a couple of hours and focus on family, friends, and food.

For those fortunate enough to have passed bowls of comfort food around a family table growing up, "Grandmother's Sunday Dinner" at Tanglewood will transport you to that space, whether your memory extends to the 2020s or the 1920s. The best qualities of Southern hospitality are on full display, dressed up in soul-warming details, like checkered tablecloths, creaky wooden chairs, patterned dishes straight from Grandma's cupboard, and old *Saturday Evening Post* covers framed on the wall.

Owners Anne and Jim Hardwick agree with the sense of timelessness at their restaurant, with one qualifier: "I think the food we're serving now is the best we've ever made," Anne says. That may be true, but the bottomless bowls of buttermilk biscuits, cornbread, cole slaw, green beans, black-eyed peas, mashed potatoes, fried chicken, pulled pork, and country ham comprise the same lineup that was dished out when the doors opened nearly 40 years ago.

Contributing to the idyllic Virginia vibe is the history of the property, which is as rich as the brownie sundae that closes out your meal. The cabin itself was built in 1928, and at different points over the years, it has functioned as a gas station/sandwich shop and community gathering spot for concerts, weekly dances, and the annual Goochland High School senior prom. Tanglewood feels like a collection of old memories, yet every weekend new ones are still being generated. The next time the modern world gets you down, just drive west for a dose of nostalgia and more country fixins than you can shake a stick at.

Address 2210 River Road W, Maidens, VA 23102, +1 (804) 556-3284, https://tanglewood-ordinary-country-restaurant.square.site | Getting there By car, take I-64 West to exit 175 onto SR-288 South, then take the exit onto W Creek Parkway then turn right onto Patterson Avenue | Hours Fri 4:30–8pm, Sat 4:30–9pm, Sat noon–7pm | Tip If you're feeling fancy, trade in the checkered tablecloth for a white one and head downtown to Julep's for an elevated take on Southern classics, like fried green tomatoes and shrimp & grits (420 E Grace Street, https://juleps.net).

97 — Texas Beach Skate Park
Epicenter of Richmond's DIY skateboarding scene

In the 2023 documentary *Greetings From Richmond*, part of a Red Bull-sponsored series highlighting the skateboarding scene in cities around the globe, director Jonathan Mehring interviewed stakeholders about what makes the city special. Words that popped up in the interviews were "gritty," "lawless," and, repeatedly, "crusty," the term for the type of unpolished, weathered terrain, where, Jonquil Moore, one local skater featured in the documentary, puts it, "You really have to, like, stick it or you're gonna eat shit."

Texas Beach Skate Park, also called Treasure Island for reasons no one seems to know, epitomizes the DIY culture among Richmond skaters. Notable for a protracted battle that earned the subculture legitimacy in the eyes of the city, the park has been shaped over the years, quite literally, by the hands of the skateboarders themselves. What started off as an abandoned, concrete slab became a community project, into which local skaters have poured their blood, sweat, and tears, along with the tons of concrete that now form its bowls and quarter-pipes.

The city silently tolerated the takeover of the space until 2017, when, after years of tension and compromise, local government officials formally recognized Texas Beach as a skate park and approved its expansion. Enhancements would still be funded and carried out by the volunteers who built it up from the original slab, but now with recognition of the increasingly diverse skate scene as an asset to the broader community, rather than a nuisance.

Even if you don't skate, you can pull up a crappy plastic chair and enjoy watching thrashers of all ages, genders, and hues drop into the bowl at Texas Beach. The rattle of the ball bearings on a long carve and the pop of the wheels running over the cope are oddly soothing unless, of course, the rider catches a crusty edge and eats it.

Address 1907 Treasure Island Trail, Richmond, VA 23220 | Getting there Bus 78 to Pennsylvania Avenue & Carter Street | Hours Daily dusk–dawn | Tip For those needing gear or directions to hidden skating venues like the River Bowl, visit Carytown's Venue Skateboards and chat with owner Maury Blankinship, de facto godfather of the Richmond skate scene (2926 W Cary Street, www.venueskateboards.com).

98 Ti Ameny Net

Pay a visit to an Egyptian lady

Sometime between 685 and 525 BC, a wealthy Egyptian woman in her early 30s died. She was placed in an ornate coffin and laid to rest in a tomb near Thebes, a city along the banks of the Nile. She remained undisturbed for approximately 2500 years until her tomb was exhumed in 1869. After changing hands several times, her remains and her coffin were purchased by Professor J. L. M. Curry (1825–1903) to display in the new antiquities museum at Richmond College. In 1897 an Egyptologist interpreted the markings on her coffin, and identified her by the name "Ti Ameny Net."

Her journey from Thebes to the Ancient World Gallery, where she currently resides, was somewhat circuitous. She and 29 other mummies were gifted to the Prince of Wales (1841–1910), who gave the remains of Ti Ameny Net to his translator, who then sold them to Professor Curry while he was relic-hunting in Egypt in 1875. Unable to front the costs of her transport Stateside, Curry negotiated travel by way of the 1876 Centennial Exposition in Philadelphia. Finally, in December 1876, she arrived in Richmond, where she's been ever since.

Ti Ameny Net now rests safely behind two inches of plexiglass at the Ancient World Gallery, a quiet, cozy room tucked between the offices of professors and study spaces on the fourth floor of the Humanities Building. In the last two decades, curators in the Department of Classics have restored the mummy and her coffin and commissioned research, including a CT scan, to learn about her and the society in which she lived.

In 2010, the gallery adopted a policy of declining artifacts without a recorded provenance prior to 1970, when UNESCO passed regulations to prevent improper acquisition of cultural property. In contrast to some past displays of mummified remains, the curators have ensured that Ti Ameny Net is treated with dignity in accordance with modern standards.

Address 410 Westhampton Way, Humanities Building, Room 409, Richmond, VA 23173, +1 (804) 289-8736, classics.richmond.edu/gallery/index.html | Getting there Bus 77 to Richmond Way & UR Students Commons | Hours Mon–Fri 10am–noon & 1:30–4:30pm while school is in session; by appointment only during summer months | Tip The most beautiful place on what the *Princeton Review* called the country's most beautiful college campus in 2024 is the wooden gazebo on an island in the middle of Westhampton Lake at the University of Richmond. Per campus legend, two students who kiss on the gazebo are destined to marry, unless one pushes the other into the lake (410 Westhampton Way, www.richmond.edu).

99 Tom Wolfe's Childhood Home

"The perfect place to grow up"

In 1991, the writer Tom Wolfe (1930–2018) penned a letter to the then-owner of his childhood home. It opens thusly: "I can scarcely tell you what a pleasure it was to see that picture of 3307 Gloucester Road. To this day I dream about that house."

The house is a typical, Cape Cod-style, Northside home, neither intrinsically remarkable nor necessarily so for the fact that Wolfe lived there. The street is worth a visit simply to put into context the love letter Wolfe wrote about his boyhood home so many decades later.

Written in the prose that Wolfe used to change American literature, but exchanging his hallmark cynicism with a sincerity reserved for childhood nostalgia, he describes his memories of the house, which his father built in the early 1930s. He recalls looking out his second-story window, the one all the way to the left when looking from Gloucester, at the fireworks from the State Fair and falling asleep to the sounds of the trains in the Acca yards. "I used to find the sounds very romantic," he wrote.

The letter also lyricizes the Sherwood Forest neighborhood, which he calls "absolute paradise for children." He treasured his boyhood memories, like pickup baseball at the local sandlot, heading to the State Fair with twelve nickels and a parental imperative to be home by supper, and "riding our bicycles, balloon-tire, of course, along Loxley Road at night while the fireflies twinkled among the mimosa blossoms … [W]hat I will always remember are the freedom, confidence, and unfettered pleasure that we children had."

Wolfe's parents lived in the house until 1957, five years before he headed to New York, destined to become a dapper, cosmopolitan, white-suit-clad fixture on the Manhattan social scene. The letter makes evident that he never forgot his Richmond roots.

Address 3307 Gloucester Road, Richmond, VA 23227 | Getting there Bus 1 to Chamberlayne & Rennie Avenues | Hours Unrestricted from the outside only | Tip At the same time that Wolfe was gallivanting around Sherwood Park, two future Hollywood legends were doing the same two neighborhoods north in Bellevue. Oscar-winning siblings Shirley MacLaine and Warren Beatty grew up in the American foursquare at 3954 Fauquier Avenue.

100 Tombstone House
Virginia's most bizarre home

Petersburg's Poplar Grove National Cemetery was founded in 1866 by a federal commission seeking to relocate the remains of approximately 5,000 Union soldiers killed in combat in the Siege of Petersburg that ended the Civil War. Short on time and manpower in the wake of these bloody battles, fellow soldiers hastily buried the men in slipshod graveyards strewn throughout the area. The commission brought them together after the war for a proper burial.

In the throes of the Great Depression, the cemetery was having a hard time making ends meet. To make some quick cash, management removed the upright marble tombstones, cut them in half, laid the top halves flat over the graves, and sold the bottom halves. Who, you may inquire, would want the bottom halves of 2,200 tombstones? Another graveyard? A sculptor chiseling an army of tiny busts? No. The purchaser in question was a resourceful man named Oswald Young, who paid $45 for the marble slabs, from which in 1933 he built the house in 1933, still standing at 1736 Youngs Road.

From the road, the structure is relatively nondescript, a modest building with a simple design. You would likely not glance twice at it without knowing its history. Looking closer though, it's impossible to separate the whole from its building blocks, each of which once memorialized the life of an individual man. Contrasting the accepted provenance of the stones, there are rumors that a few of them do bear the names of a soldier but that these were plastered over and were placed facing inwards.

There are gardens around the house with flowers providing a dash of color against the white marble and a pop of cheer to offset the somber overtones. Alas, the camellias and mums have not sufficiently stifled the perception that the house is haunted, though it's hard to imagine how 2,200 ghosts could possibly all inhabit this one modest abode, no matter how hauntable it may be.

Address 1736 Youngs Road, Petersburg, VA 23803 | Getting there By car, take I-95 South to exit 51 onto I-85 South to exit 65, turn right onto Squirrel Level Road to the destination; bus PAT Freedom Express to Petersburg Transfer Station, then Lee Avenue bus to Halcun Drive & Youngs Road | Hours Unrestricted from the outside only | Tip If you want to learn more about the men whose tombstones built the house and the other 620,000 who paid the ultimate sacrifice, visit Petersburg's National Museum of the Civil War Soldier (6125 Boydton Plank Road, Petersburg, www.pamplinpark.org/things-to-do/national-museum-civil-war-soldier).

101 Trapezium House

A new slant on an old classic

Petersburg was once the third-largest city in Virginia and a flourishing center of commerce, which remains evident in the diverse array of prominent buildings leftover from its heyday. The Greek Revival style is represented by the magnificent Hustings Courthouse and the Exchange Building. A pair of plantation homes from the mid-1700s, Battersea and Mayfield, are built in the Palladian and Georgian styles, respectively. The A.L. Scott House and a few other residences exemplify the boom in Italianate architecture in the 1850s.

The Federalist style, however, is the quintessential architecture of Petersburg. When a fire destroyed two-thirds of the city in 1815, much of Old Towne was rebuilt in the Federalist style, with its clean lines, symmetry, and vibrant brickwork. Classic examples still standing include Centre Hill mansion, the Nathaniel Friend House, and Farmers Bank. There's one Federalist structure in Petersburg, though, that stands out from the others: the Trapezium House.

Built in 1817 by an Irish merchant named Charles O'Hara, the three-story Trapezium House looks similar to its Federalist neighbors, but for one distinct feature. None of its walls meet at 90-degree angles. Legend has it that when Mr. O'Hara was designing his house, his West Indian servant convinced him that evil spirits take up residence in the 90-degree angles of a home. To avoid the risk of being haunted, the superstitious O'Hara had his house built as a trapezoid, with acute or obtuse angles in every corner. The result is a mind-bending display of odd geometry.

The structure was previously a museum, which welcomed visitors to behold more of O'Hara's eccentric design on the interior: staircases, mantels, door frames, and lintels all avoiding the right angles in one way or another. Nowadays, Trapezium House is an apartment building whose quirkiness can only be appreciated from the street.

Address 244 N Market Street, Petersburg, VA 23803 | Getting there By car, take I-95 to E Washington Street exit in Petersburg, turn right onto N Market Street | Hours Unrestricted from outside only | Tip In homage to the eccentric building a few blocks west, Petersburg's premier taphouse is named Trapezium Brewing Company. Built into an old 1870s ice and coal factory, sipping suds under the red umbrellas is a must on a visit to the Cockade City (423 N 3rd Street, Petersburg, www.trapeziumbrewing.com).

102 Tsarevich Egg
A vestige of Russian royalty

Every Easter between 1894 and 1918, Tsar Nicholas II (1868–1918) presented his wife and mother each with one egg designed by Peter Carl Fabergé (1846–1920). Of the 52 so-called Imperial eggs, five reside at the Virginia Museum of Fine Arts, the largest collection of these priceless artifacts outside of Russia. Each of the eggs held some special meaning for its recipient, but the 1912 rendition, an egg carved of bright blue lapis lazuli encased in gold framework, was particularly prized by Nicholas's wife, the Tsarina Alexandra (1872–1918).

The egg was called "Tsarevich," Russian for "heir to the tsar," referring to Nicholas's son Alexei, who was famously afflicted with the bleeding disorder hemophilia B. While the family was on vacation in Poland in the Fall of 1912, Alexei sustained a life-threatening hemorrhage in his thigh and abdomen. His health deteriorated so profoundly that a priest delivered the boy's last sacrament, and the Royal Court completed his death certificate. The next day, Grigori Rasputin (1869–1916), one of the few people outside of the royal family aware of the situation, correctly prophesied that "the little one will not die." Shortly thereafter, Alexei began to recover, allowing Rasputin to fix his strained relationship with the Tsarina and regain influence over the Romanovs. Another insider privy to the incident was Fabergé, who designed the egg that year as a tribute to the boy's miraculous recovery.

In 1933, the Antikvariat, a commission established by Vladimir Lenin (1870–1924) and carried forward by Josef Stalin (1878–1973) to liquidate Russian treasures for desperately needed cash, sold 30 of the 52 Imperial eggs, including Tsarevich. Along with four other eggs, it ended up in the hands of Lillian Thomas Pratt (1876–1947), who bequeathed her entire collection to the VMFA, where they are on permanent display, free of charge.

Address 200 N Arthur Ashe Boulevard, Richmond, VA 23220, +1 (804) 340-1400, www.vmfa.museum, info@vmfa.museum | Getting there Bus 20 to Robinson Street & Hanover Avenue or bus 77 to Grove Avenue & N Arthur Ashe Boulevard | Hours Sat–Tue 10am–5pm, Wed–Fri 10am–9pm | Tip A more recent addition to the Richmond art scene is the Institute of Contemporary Art on the campus of Virginia Commonwealth University, which hosts an ever changing lineup of exhibits, performances, and films (601 W Broad Street, www.icavcu.org).

103 Tuckahoe Schoolhouse
Where Jefferson learned to read and write

Tuckahoe Plantation certainly doesn't feel like a tourist attraction. There's no front desk, no name-tagged gents, and no *grande dames* in 18th-century costumes to welcome you. There are some little placards tacked up here and there for a self-guided tour, but otherwise it feels like you're wandering around someone's countryside home, which, in fact, you are. A mud-splattered truck rumbles by en route to the working horse stables. There's a baby pool sitting beside the manor house. The overlay of modern banality with historic eminence is itself remarkable, as is the plantation's accessibility by the public.

Almost as old as the Old Dominion itself, Tuckahoe Plantation was founded in 1714, when a prominent colonial planter named Thomas Randolph (1683–1729) settled on the sprawling estate in what is now Goochland County. Randolph's son, William, inherited the property, where he built the aforementioned mansion and started a family there in the 1730s. By 1745, both William and his wife had died unexpectedly, but before his death, he arranged for his friend Peter Jefferson to move to Tuckahoe, along with his wife and two-year-old son Thomas to oversee the plantation and raise the Randolph children. In his will, he also left money for the construction of a one-room schoolhouse adjacent to the plantation mansion. This small structure, which still stands, is where a young Thomas Jefferson (1743–1826) learned to read and write.

In an effort to cool down the classroom during the humid Virginia summers, the ceiling was built as a dome and would have likely been the first such structure that Jefferson ever saw. One may speculate that the ceiling on this simple schoolhouse influenced his admiration for domes and inspired their use much later in the architectural masterpieces he designed, such as Monticello and the Rotunda at the University of Virginia.

Address 12601 River Road, Richmond, VA 23238, +1 (804) 971-8329, www.tuckahoeplantation.com, HistoricTuckahoeTours@gmail.com | Getting there By car, take Cary Street Road west to River Road to the destination | Hours Daily 9am–5pm | Tip The First Freedom Center features a large statue of Jefferson and commemorates his signing of the Virginia Statute for Religious Freedom when he was governor of the Commonwealth. The document served as a template for the religious freedom clause in the Bill of Rights (14 S 14th Street, www.thevalentine.org/exhibition/first-freedom-center).

104 Union Seminary Gargoyle

Vigilant guardian of Morton Library

A warning to any evil spirits in Richmond intending to take harbor in Morton Library at the Union Presbyterian Seminary: Beware the gargoyle guarding the entrance. With his claws and pointy ears, the little terracotta goblin fits the mold of a typical Gothic grotesque. His wire-rimmed reading glasses and well-manicured, parted coiffe, though, seem more befitting a crotchety librarian warding off scofflaws who would dare talk above a whisper in the stacks or flout the return dates of their borrowed books.

Indeed, the gargoyle bears a striking resemblance to the late longtime librarian John Trotti, who worked for the institution from 1968 until 2002. Trotti was by all accounts a caring and beloved character at the library. He was also a gargoyle enthusiast, having placed several of them in his garden at home. According to Rex Springston of the *Richmond Times-Dispatch*, when advocating for the renovation of the campus' library, Trotti joked that he would "go upstairs and stick my head out and be the gargoyle." In homage to the longtime librarian, Union Seminary President Louis Weeks commissioned local sculptor B Millner to create the gargoyle in Trotti's likeness. At a ceremony in 2003 the gargoyle was unveiled to Trotti's surprise and delight.

The library that the gargoyle guards is magnificent. Half of the building is the original Schauffler Hall, which opened in 1922 as part chapel and part classroom for the instruction of worship at the seminary. The other half was added onto the existing structure in 1997, forming a four-story atrium. Its Gothic arches prop up a vaulted glass ceiling that illuminates the space below, consisting of the old red brick wall, the new oak wall, and oriental rugs over a gray slate floor. Visitors pure of spirit will be undeterred by the librarian-gargoyle and may enter to find a beautiful, peaceful space to study.

Address 3401 Brook Road, Richmond, VA 23227, +1 (800) 229-2990, https://library.upsem.edu | Getting there Bus 1 to Chamberlayne & Melrose | Hours See website for seasonal hours | Tip Just up the road from the Union Seminary in Bellevue is Enoteca Sogno, the coziest hole-in-the-wall, date-night restaurant in Richmond (1223 Bellevue Avenue, www.enoteca-sogno.com).

105 Valentine's Meat Juice

The proteinaceous potion that launched a dynasty

In 1870, a Richmond woman named Ann Valentine fell gravely ill with what was described as "a severe and protracted derangement of the organs of digestion." As she deteriorated over the course of several weeks and physicians declared that nothing more could be done, her husband, a dry-good salesman and amateur chemist named Mann S. Valentine began working furiously to concoct a mixture of egg whites and reduced beef juice. Ann took the first dose of the elixir on New Year's Eve 1870, and gradually regained her strength over the next few weeks. When news of Ann's recovery spread across Richmond, Mann realized the commercial potential of his tonic, and thus was born the global phenomenon known as Valentine's Meat Juice.

Within a few years, the tonic became accepted by the medical establishment and filled the shelves of the pharmacies nationwide. In 1874, Valentine published a booklet of endorsements from physicians across the nation swearing by its benefits. The product exploded internationally after Valentine represented Virginia at the Paris Exposition in 1878. Famous adopters of the late 19th century included Chinese viceroy Li Hung Chang, King of England George V, Emperor Yoshita of Japan, and, during recovery from an assassination attempt to which he eventually succumbed, President James A. Garfield.

The tonic earned Valentine a fortune, some of which he bequeathed to the establishment of Richmond's first museum at his downtown mansion upon his death in 1893. Known these days simply as the Valentine, the museum tells the 400-year history of the City of Richmond. Some incredible artifacts are housed there including: a pre-European dugout canoe; the shackles of an enslaved Virginian; the smashed and graffitied statue of Jefferson Davis; one of author Tom Wolfe's patented white linen suits; and, of course, a tiny bottle of the potion that launched it all.

Address 1015 East Clay Street, Richmond, VA 23219, +1 (804) 649-0711, www.thevalentine.org, info@thevalentine.org | Getting there Bus 1A, 1B, 1C, 7A, 7B, 56 to Broad & 12th Streets | Hours Tue & Wed, Fri–Sun 10am–5pm, Thu 10am–7pm | Tip Parked right out front of the Valentine, the Caribbean Grill food cart serves up heaps of Trinidadian fare, like jerk chicken and curried oxtail, with plantains and cabbage. Among a fleet of food carts near the VCU medical school, Philmore Moses' ode to his Caribbean cuisine leads the pack (1009 East Clay Street).

106 Vinyl Conflict Records
Wax for the masses

Owner of Vinyl Conflict, Bobby Egger, recognizes that for the casual music fan, the record store can be an intimidating space. Recall the scene from *High Fidelity* (2000) in which an ornery employee excoriates a trench coat-sporting older gent for his "terrible taste" after he requests a Stevie Wonder album. Perhaps it is that acknowledgement that allows Vinyl Conflict, despite the relative obscurity of its collection and the vast knowledge of its staff, to shed the stereotype and sell records without a hint of pretense.

The shop opened in 2008 as only the second record store in the city, and much has changed since then. Egger took the reins in 2012. The store moved from Oregon Hill to downtown in 2022. The number of record stores in Richmond grew to double digits. Despite the changes, the store's original mission remains the same: to provide a marketplace for underappreciated music. Vinyl Conflict values local artists in particular and has its own label that has supported 35 bands over the years, all from Richmond.

The diversity of the collection has expanded as well. DIY punk and metal still occupy a large share of the shelf space, but Egger says there aren't really boundaries around what the store sells. "We definitely have some albums from major labels… If a kid comes in asking for Taylor Swift, we'll talk to them about it; otherwise they'll never come back into a record store." All are welcome, whether they seek mainstream music or the deep cut on the B-side of the demo of a Midlothian garage band.

Egger also seeks to restore the richness that record collecting has lost to modern conveniences. "There is an 'Amazonication,' to collecting these days," he says. "People click the button and check out. We want you to come and dig in, browse the rack, talk to us, let us play an album. Tell us what you want, what you like. You'll be surprised what you'll find."

Address 300 E Grace Street, Richmond, VA 23219, +1 (804) 644-2555,
www.vinylconflict.com | Getting there Bus 1, 2A, 2B, 2C, 3C, 14, 78 to 4th & Broad Streets |
Hours Tue–Sat 11am–7pm, Sun & Mon noon–6pm | Tip For metalheads in search of live
music, one of the better local mosh pits can be found at Canal Club, a large, brick warehouse
that originally housed the Old Dominion Hide & Fur Company in the 1800s (1545 E Cary
Street, www.thecanalclub.com).

107 Virago Spirits

Booze of great stature, strength, and courage

By the time Brad Haneberg seriously considered leaving his career as an attorney to open a brewery, a dream he and his brothers had entertained for years, it felt too late; the Richmond craft brew market had become saturated. Then one day, like a gift from Bacchus, the Roman god of alcohol, a giant wooden box arrived unexpectedly on his doorstep. When he pried open the crate, there sat a handmade copper still, and in the tradition of Prohibition-era Virginians before him, Haneberg got to work experimenting with homemade spirits.

After some formal distilling courses, Haneberg teamed up with his wife Vicky and two brothers, Barry and Barton, and the four founded Virago Spirits. The name Virago is both a clever mashup of *Vir*ginia and Chic*ago*, wherefrom the Hanebergs migrated, and a noun meaning "a woman of great stature, strength, and courage." Vicky expounds on the definition thusly: "To us, it means a person who doesn't let society define who they are."

Bucking the trend of bourbon production that swept the nation in the early 2000s, the Hanebergs chose instead to make rum and gin. "Barry has a special place in his heart for misunderstood spirits," Vicky remembers. "Bourbon was being heralded as the unofficial spirit of America, but people forget that rum was here first." As for the gin, "most people that hate gin have probably only had a dry London gin that tastes like a pinecone."

The tasting room is a beautiful space, covered in murals on all four walls, a virago on three of them, and, on the fourth, floral patterns made of the ingredients that go into the spirits. A cozy, wooden bar sits in one corner next to a huge glass window looking out onto the production space with its enormous red still, a maker of French cognac in a past life. The owners welcome the public on tours of the production space on the third Wednesday of each month.

Address 1727 Rhoadmiller Street, Richmond, VA 23220, +1 (804) 355-8746, www.viragospirits.com | Getting there Bus 14 to Hermitage Road & Rhoadmiller Street | Hours Wed 10am–5pm, Thu 4pm–9:30pm, Fri & Sat 2–9:30pm, Sun 2–6pm | Tip The bourbon Renaissance came to Richmond in 2008 with Reservoir, only the third bourbon distillery outside of Kentucky since Prohibition. Visit the oaky tasting room in Scott's Addition to sample their superb spirits (1800A Summit Avenue, www.reservoirdistillery.com).

108 __ Virginia Motorsports Park

Next-level speed at Richmond's "other" raceway

In the world of American auto racing, stock car racing and NASCAR, its behemoth governing body, get most of the attention. This is no less true in Richmond, home to the world-renowned Richmond Raceway, a venue as storied as the sport itself. That said, the subculture of Richmond-area motorheads who frequent the Virginia Motorsports Parkway (VMP) challenge the assumption that NASCAR is king.

Located just south of Petersburg in North Dinwiddie County, the VMP is a complex of venues that host various racing events. There's a dirt track with big jumps that motorbikes and BMX bikes fly over. There's the "Dirtplex," a giant mud pit that tractors and big-wheeled monsters must splash through as quickly as possible. The centerpiece of the complex, though, is the quarter-mile strip that hosts drag racers of several varieties. The venue is a National Hot Rod Association (NHRA) partner track, which the owners promote as "the world's premier drag racing facility with the smoothest and flattest racing surface on the planet." The site participates in big-time competitions, including the NHRA Nationals.

The top fuel dragster is a 25-foot-long, pencil-thin, rear-engined drag-racing car that accelerates from 0 to 100 mph in less than a second, reaches speeds of 335 mph, and completes a 1,000-foot course in 3.5 seconds. Watching one take off at the VMP feels like watching a fighter jet take off from an aircraft carrier as it fades off into the distance before you even see the tree turn green. The sensations produced by the combustion of nitro in these engines – the intense rumble through the bleachers into your gut, the smell of aerosolized rubber after each burnout, the scream of the engine like a banshee with a megaphone – are staggering. Races take place most weekends from March through November. Bring your own ear protection!

Address 8018 Boydton Plank Road, North Dinwiddie, VA 23803, +1 (804) 862-3174, https://racevmp.com, info@racevmp.com | Getting there By car, take I-95 South to exit 51 on I-85 South, then take exit 61 on US-460 West, turn left onto Airport Street, and right onto Boydton Plank Road | Hours Mon–Thu 9am–6pm, Fri 9am–5pm, Sat 1–5pm | Tip No one takes farm-to-table more literally than the farmers at Richlands Dairy & Creamery, where visitors can watch how their ice cream is made from udder to cone. The farm is a hike from Richmond but worth it for the freshest ice cream and chocolate milk (460 Cox Road, Wilsons, www.richlandsdairyfarm.com).

109 Visual Arts Center
Hub for the city's creatives

In 1963, seven Richmonders opened a studio in Church Hill called the Hand Workshop.

Sixty-plus years have passed, and although the name, location, and offerings have changed, the center's mission remains the same: Community artists share studio space, teach classes, and display their art for the public.

As the Visual Arts Center (aka VisArts) has grown, its reach has increased significantly. By the numbers, each year 220 teachers host 40,000 people in 1,500 classes within 17 studios dedicated to 12 artistic media: clay, creative writing, digital, drawing and painting, fiber, flameworking, glass, letterpress, metals, photography, printmaking, and wood.

Despite a mammoth operation, each class feels like an intimate get-together. Some of the art produced is serious, such as complex scarves woven on rigid heddle looms, glass jewelry forged with blowtorches, paper mâché parade floats the size of SUVs. Many of these pieces will go on to be featured in the large, first-floor exhibition space. Other creations are seriously silly. For example there's a course called "Fun Sculpey Putty Fridge Magnets," in which a teacher dumps a small mountain of mashable clay into the center of a table, and for 75 minutes, strangers sit together, making small talk and molding little refrigerator magnets. Through countless interactions like these, the Visual Arts Center has become the hub for community arts in Richmond.

With several programs specifically for young artists, the center is particularly welcoming to children. These include "Art After School," weekly classes for kids aged 6–14, and "Art League," providing more intensive instruction to high schoolers trying to put together a portfolio. True to its motto, "Art for Everyone. Creativity for Life," the center also has a robust financial aid program to make its offerings accessible to all Richmonders.

Address 1812 W Main Street, Richmond, VA 23220, +1 (804) 353-0094, www.visarts.org | Getting there Bus 5, 77 to Main Street & Allen Avenue | Hours Daily 9am–9pm | Tip Catty-corner to VisArts, you will find cheap, delicious Salvadoran fare at El Pope. Dollar-for-dollar, the *pupusas* are among the best food in Richmond (1731 W Main Street, www.facebook.com/ElPopeCosina).

110 White House of the Confederacy

Relic of wartime Richmond

There is no documentation of Abraham Lincoln and Jefferson Davis ever meeting, but the two seemed to have been linked by fate. They were both born in Kentucky, less than a year apart. They overlapped in Congress for nearly two years and spent most of the Civil War as bitter foes, living 120 miles from one another. At the close of the war in early April 1865, the two just missed each other at 1201 East Clay Street, an address also known as the White House of the Confederacy.

During the evening of April 2, as the remaining Confederates set fire to the city, Davis left his home and hopped a southbound train out of Richmond. Around noon on April 4, Lincoln ascended the front stairs of the mansion amid a triumphant crowd made up in large part of recently liberated Black citizens. The president sat in Davis' easy chair and requested a glass of water. Everyone else passed around a bottle of Davis' whiskey. Lincoln and General Godfrey Weitzel (1835 – 1884) proceeded to the small parlor in the northwest corner. The president left the mansion after lunch and the next day returned to Washington, DC.

These days, the public can still visit the house, which looks much as it did in 1865, though in a much different setting. Surrounded on three sides by high-rises that comprise the VCU Medical Center, the modern world has grown up around the mansion. For much of the 20th century, the space was used as a reliquary to the Lost Cause, with each room representing a different Confederate state and jammed to the gills with uniforms, locks of hair, and faded "stars and bars" banners. Under the management of the American Civil War Museum, which has furnished the house with authentic decor and possessions of the Davis family, tours of the house now intend to educate rather than glorify.

Address 1201 E Clay Street, Richmond, VA 23219, +1 (804) 649-1861,
www.acwm.org/white-house-of-the-confederacy | Getting there Bus 5, 12 to Leigh & 11th
Streets | Hours Tue–Thu 11am–4pm, Fri–Mon 10:30am–4pm | Tip Around the block
sits the First Baptist Church, which was designed by Thomas Walter, architect of the US
Capitol. Now a student commons for the VCU medical campus, the space was used as a
Confederate Hospital (1110 E Broad Street, thecommons.vcu.edu/where-to-go/hunton-
student-center-mcv-campus).

111__ Wolf Creek Tribal Center

The native perspective on Virginia history

For all the effort that Richmond devotes to its remarkable history, the majority of those efforts only covers about 2% of the roughly 15,000 years that humans have lived in what is called Virginia today, and that's the 2% that has occurred since the arrival of Europeans to this continent. But the Wolf Creek Tribal Center, the community gathering place for the Cherokee people of Virginia, is one place where Richmonders can learn about Native American culture, both ancient and contemporary.

On Saturdays, the tribe's current leader Chief Terry Price welcomes guests to the Center, where you can learn about Cherokee culture through the artifacts on display, such as tools made from stone and pots made from clay. Modern aspects of life are represented by artwork and regalia worn for powwows with other tribes. Chief Terry hosts a drum circle on the third Tuesday of every month, where he passes down stories to young members of the tribe through music. The center also periodically organizes archaeological digs on nearby property that is rich in native artifacts. Community members are invited to participate.

One aspect of the Tribal Center unique to the Cherokee of Virginia is its focus on their ongoing struggle for recognition by the Commonwealth. What little attention local museums devote to Indigenous culture generally goes to the Algonquian-speaking tribes descended from the Powhatan Confederation. The Cherokee effort has been particularly challenging because the Iroquoian-speaking Wolf Creek Cherokee had a smaller presence in the mountains of Southwest Virginia, and they relied on oral tradition rather than written documentation, not to mention efforts by bureaucrats to remove Native American heritage from the Census. The Cherokee have petitioned for years to be recognized by the State, but thus far these requests have been denied.

Address 7400 Osborne Turnpike, Richmond, VA 23231, +1 (804) 387-0655, www.wolfcreekcherokee.com | Getting there By car, take E Main or Dock Streets west to the Old Osborne Turnpike to the destination | Hours Sat 11am–3pm | Tip For more information on Pre-Columbian Virginia and Native culture, travel to the larger but further afield Pamunkey Indian Museum & Cultural Center, about an hour east of Richmond (175 Lay Landing Road, King William, www.pamunkey.org/museum-cultural-center).

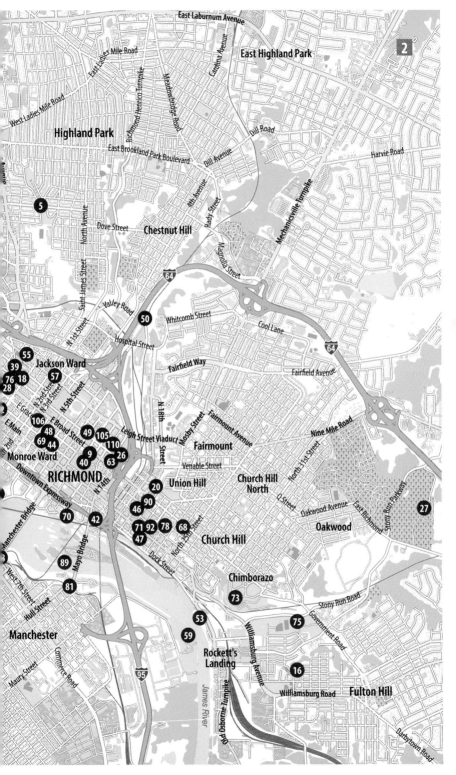

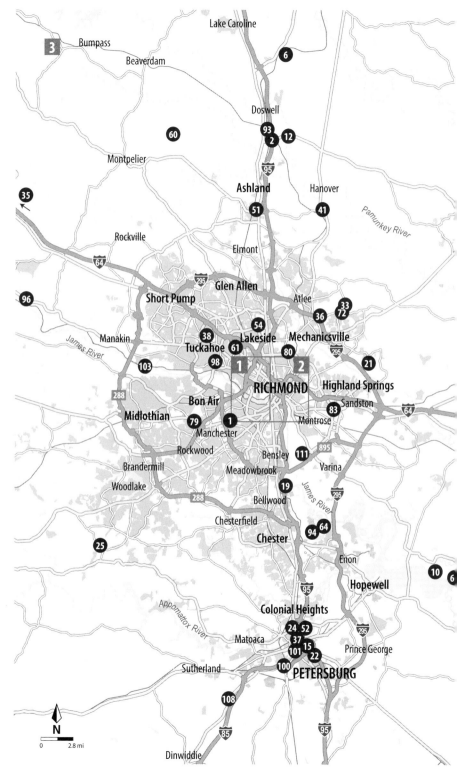

Andrea Seiger, John Dean
**111 Places in Washington
That You Must Not Miss**
ISBN 978-3-7408-2399-3

Lauri Williamson, David Wardrick
**111 Places in Black Culture
in Washington, DC That You
Must Not Miss**
ISBN 978-3-7408-2003-9

Kaitlin Calogera, Rebecca Grawl,
Cynthia Schiavetto
**111 Places in Women's
History in Washington
That You Must Not Miss**
ISBN 978-3-7408-1590-5

Allison Robicelli, John Dean
**111 Places in Baltimore
That You Must Not Miss**
ISBN 978-3-7408-1696-4

Brandon Schultz, Lucy Baber
**111 Places in Philadelphia
That You Must Not Miss**
ISBN 978-3-7408-1376-5

Jo-Anne Elikann, Susan Lusk
**111 Places in New York
That You Must Not Miss**
ISBN 978-3-7408-2400-6

Evan Levy, Rachel Mazor,
Joost Heijmenberg
**111 Places for Kids in New York
That You Must Not Miss**
ISBN 978-3-7408-1993-4

Wendy Lubovich,
Ed Lefkowicz
**111 Museums in New York
That You Must Not Miss**
ISBN 978-3-7408-2374-0

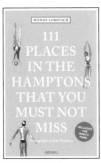

Wendy Lubovich,
Jean Hodgens
**111 Places in the Hamptons
That You Must Not Miss**
ISBN 978-3-7408-1891-3

Kim Windyka, Heather Kapplow,
Alyssa Wood
**111 Places in Boston
That You Must Not Miss**
ISBN 978-3-7408-2056-5

Brian Hayden, Jesse Pitzler
**111 Places in Buffalo
That You Must Not Miss**
ISBN 978-3-7408-2151-7

Amy Bizzarri, Susie Inverso
**111 Places in Chicago
That You Must Not Miss**
ISBN 978-3-7408-2402-0

Michelle Madden,
Janet McMillan
**111 Places in Milwaukee
That You Must Not Miss**
ISBN 978-3-7408-1643-8

Travis Swann Taylor
**111 Places in Atlanta
That You Must Not Miss**
ISBN 978-3-7408-1887-6

Dana DuTerroil, Joni Fincham,
Daniel Jackson
**111 Places in Houston
That You Must Not Miss**
ISBN 978-3-7408-2265-1

Dana DuTerroil, Joni Fincham,
Sara S. Murphy
**111 Places for Kids in Houston
That You Must Not Miss**
ISBN 978-3-7408-2267-5

Kelsey Roslin, Nic Yeager,
Jesse Pitzler
**111 Places in Austin
That You Must Not Miss**
ISBN 978-3-7408-1642-1

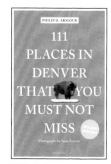

Philip D. Armour,
Susie Inverso
**111 Places in Denver
That You Must Not Miss**
ISBN 978-3-7408-1220-1

Susan Veness,
Simon Veness, Kayla Smith
111 Places in Orlando
That You Must Not Miss
ISBN 978-3-7408-1900-2

Cristyle Egitto, Jakob Takos
111 Places in Palm Beach
That You Must Not Miss
ISBN 978-3-7408-2398-6

Travis Swann Taylor
111 Places in Phoenix
That You Must Not Miss
ISBN 978-3-7408-2050-3

Laurel Moglen, Julia Posey,
Lyudmila Zotova
111 Places in Los Angeles
That You Must Not Miss
ISBN 978-3-7408-1889-0

Brian Joseph
111 Places in Hollywood
That You Must Not Miss
ISBN 978-3-7408-1819-7

Floriana Petersen, Steve Werney
111 Places in San Francisco
That You Must Not Miss
ISBN 978-3-7408-2058-9

Floriana Petersen, Steve Werney
111 Places in Napa and
Sonoma That You Must
Not Miss
ISBN 978-3-7408-1553-0

Floriana Petersen, Steve Werney
111 Places in Silicon Valley
That You Must Not Miss
ISBN 978-3-7408-1346-8

Harriet Baskas, Cortney Kelley
111 Places in Seattle
That You Must Not Miss
ISBN 978-3-7408-2375-7

The process of putting together a book of this nature requires the participation of too many people to mention by name. Tending to each of these 111 places are people that work tirelessly to make their little corner of the city wonderful and collectively make Richmond such a special place. Thanks to these stewards of our River City, all of whom were incredibly generous to us with their time and effort. Many thanks to our editor Karen Seiger, who was always encouraging to this first-time writer and first-time photographer and never scolded us for our tardiness. Thanks to the world's greatest babysitters (aka Nana, Pops, Mimi, Grandpa, and Papa Charlie), to whom this book is dedicated. Thanks also to the babies themselves for their compliance in joining the "adventures" that became the stories within these entries. Lastly and most importantly, thanks to Ashley, who during the course of this project worked in the emergency department, had two children, kept our household semi-functional, *and* took the photographs that made these pages come to life, all while practicing saintly patience with my pursuits.
John Tucker

First and foremost I want to express my enormous amount of gratitude to my husband (and author) John for encouraging me to take on this project. This book that wouldn't exist without his captivating storytelling and writing. You are an inspiration. Visiting these places together has been the highlight of this project for me … especially the ones with our children in tow. Charlie, Shea, and Graham, thank you for accompanying us on many adventures around the city. For the past year, our oldest son's first question when climbing in the car would be "Are we going on an adventure?!" An immense thanks to my mom and dad, Debray and Tommy, and parents-in-law, Mary and Saint, for clocking countless hours with our kids so that we could make this happen. One of my favorite days spent working on this book was exploring historic Petersburg with my grandfather, Charlie - thanks for the company! And a huge thanks to our wonderful editor Karen for believing in me!
Ashley Tucker

John Tucker was born and raised in Richmond, where as a child, he subsisted on Ukrop's White House rolls, slept under a Richmond Braves poster, and regularly rode his bike to the Huguenot flatwater. While completing his training as an Emergency Medicine doctor in Chicago, he discovered the *111 Places* series and knew that he was destined to write the Richmond edition. Between busy shifts in the ER, John further stresses himself out by watching UVA sports and unwinds by exploring the River City with his family.

Ashley Tucker grew up in Chester, Virginia, where she received her first camera from her grandfather. After stints in New York and Chicago spent honing her photography skills, Ashley reunited with her hometown and used her camera to document Richmond's hidden treasures with her husband, the author of this book, their adventurous children, and rowdy golden retriever. When she isn't capturing the city from behind a lens, she can be found on her yoga mat at Humble Haven, spending time with her family or fixing up their vintage Richmond home.